Library of Congress Cataloging-in-Publication Data

Published by Linworth Publishing, Inc.
480 East Wilson Bridge Road, Suite L
Worthington, Ohio 43085

Copyright©1999 by Linworth Publishing, Inc.

Series Information:
        From The Professional Growth Series

ISBN 0-938865-84-6

5 4 3 2 1

Skills for Life:

Information Literacy for Grades 7-12

2nd Edition

**Christine Allen and
Mary Alice Anderson, Editors**

A Publication of THE BOOK REPORT & LIBRARY TALK
Professional Growth Series

Linworth Publishing, Inc.
Worthington, Ohio

Table of Contents

Table of Contents continued

Table of Contents continued

Acknowledgements

Linworth Publishing, Inc. wishes to thank the following library professionals for their contributions to the *Skills for Life* series:

EDITOR, GRADES K-6 AND 7-12: Christine Allen, Riverside (California) Unified School District
EDITOR, GRADES 7-12: Mary Alice Anderson, Winona (Minnesota) Middle School
CONSULTING EDITOR, GRADES K-6 AND 7-12: Judi Repman, Georgia Southern University, Statesboro, Georgia

OTHER CONTRIBUTORS:
Susan Anhold, James Madison University, Harrisonburg, Virginia
Allison Bernstein, Dale Street School, Medfield, Massachusetts
Elizabeth W. Bowen, Potomac Senior High School, Dumfries, Virginia
Kathryn K. Brown, James Madison University, Harrisonburg, Virginia
Frances Campbell, James Madison University, Harrisonburg, Virginia
Maribeth Carmichael, Sherando High School, Stephens City, Virginia
Harold Christensen, Winona (Minnesota) Middle School
Gail Dickinson, James Madison University, Harrisonburg, Virginia
Lesley S. J. Farmer, California State University at Long Beach
Chris Ebert Flench, James Madison University, Harrisonburg, Virginia
Chris Gentili, Samuels Public Library, Front Royal, Virginia
Joan Haberkorn, Fruita (Colorado) Middle School
Wanda P. Higgins, James Madison University, Harrisonburg, Virginia
Patricia Kolencik, North Clarion High School, Tionesta, Pennsylvania
Tami Little, Hinton (Iowa) Community School
Debra Kay Logan, Taft Middle School, Marion, Ohio
Jackie Mahlke, Winona (Minnesota) Middle School
Becky Mather, Mississippi Bend Area Education Agency, Bettendorf, Iowa
Donna Miller, Mesa County Valley School District 51, Grand Junction, Colorado
Lisa Muir, Islamic Saudi Academy, Fairfax, Virginia
Kate O'Grady, Winona (Minnesota) Middle School
Lisa Palkowski, Winona (Minnesota) Middle School
Shayne Russell, Mt. Laurel (New Jersey) Hartford School
Victoria Santucci, Sherando High School, Stephens City, Virginia
Rod Schwarz, Winona (Minnesota) Middle School
Dianne T. Sheetz, Signal Knob Middle School, Strasburg, Virginia
Matt Smith, Winona (Minnesota) Middle School
Barb Tibor, Winona (Minnesota) Middle School
Kathy Tobiason, The American School in Japan, Tokyo
Thom Tobiason, The American School in Japan, Tokyo
Bob Urness, Winona (Minnesota) Middle School
Joyce Kasman Valenza, Springfield Township (Pennsylvania) High School
Greg Wing, Winona (Minnesota) Middle School
Terrence E. Young, Jr., West Jefferson High School, Harvey, Louisiana
Alice Yucht, Heritage Middle School, Livingston, New Jersey

Introduction

Students today are faced with an almost totally different world than we were at their age. Beloit (Wisconsin) College faculty try each year to give everyone on staff the "big picture" regarding incoming freshman. Think about these facts in terms of your own students:

- There has been only one Pope. They can only really remember one president.
- They were nine years old when the Soviet Union broke apart and do not even recall the 'Cold War.'
- Their lifetime has always included AIDS.
- They have never had a polio shot and likely do not know what it is.
- The compact disc was introduced when they were in the womb.
- The expression "you sound like a broken record" means nothing because vinyl albums predate them, and they probably have never owned a record player.
- They have always had VCRs, but they have no idea what BETA is.
- There has always been MTV.

What does this mean to a library media specialist? Recognizing a few new basics is critical. For example, change will continue to define our world and transform the world of our students. Knowing how to learn, combined with flexibility, is the key predictor of success for our students, and their education must continue beyond their school years when they enter the world of life and work. Parents, prospective employers, and taxpayers all have new expectations of students graduating from our public schools. The national standards movement is a logical response in recognition of the need for these skills for life.

Standards are not new and are not always enthusiastically accepted. Many worry

> **Knowing how to learn, combined with flexibility, is the key predictor of success for our students...**

that just having a formal set of standards will in some way reduce the quality of the education process. But it is the way standards are utilized that will determine the quality of education, not the fact of their existence. Many national organizations have developed broad, far-reaching guidelines based on a conceptual framework for specific content areas: National Council for the Social Studies, National Council of Teachers of Mathematics, National Science Teachers Association, International Reading Association, Consortium of National Arts Education Association, International Society for Technology in Education. All these groups subscribe to the philosophy that students must be active participants in authentic learning situations. The standards for each reflect contemporary learning and information theories.

AASL and AECT developed the new edition of *Information Power: Building Partnerships for Learning* based on the goal of creating a community of lifelong learners. "Students and their learning remain at the core of library media programs and services, shaping the functions of school library media specialists. Effective teaching is today seen as a holistic process involving all aspects of student life and requiring continual assessment and feedback for meaningful learning." [1]

This change in emphasis from the earlier 1988 edition is reflected in the addition of nine information literacy standards for student learning. These standards apply to all curriculum areas, and a growing body of research shows that these competencies are directly related to student achievement. The standards consist of three categories, nine standards, and twenty-nine indicators. The three standards in the "information literacy" category

are most directly related to the services provided by the Library Media Specialist. The other two categories, "independent learning" and "social responsibility," are more general in nature, though the school library media program makes a significant contribution. Ultimately of course, graduating an information literate, productive, and responsible person is the obligation of the entire educational community.

This new edition of *Skills for Life* is organized around these nine information literacy standards in recognition of the importance of developing the fundamentals of life-long learning in students.

Lessons were solicited from library media specialists across the country, people who are working with students and teachers every day. Each guide was selectively chosen through a juried process. Instructional methods could vary but each had to have these attributes:

- Objectives are based on student standards.
- Each objective, whether process- or product-oriented, is evaluated in an explicit manner.
- Methods and content are integral to current curriculum.
- LMS and teacher(s) are co-workers with complementary roles in planning, teaching and evaluating.
- Other audiences for student products are explored when appropriate.

Each chapter focuses on one standard, with the instructional guides within that chapter emphasizing that particular standard. Many address other standards as well. Those with multiple standards were divided to achieve a balance of a grade levels, subject

> Students and their learning remain at the core of library media programs and services, shaping the functions of school library media specialists.

areas, and number of guides per chapter. Following the Table of Contents is a Correlation Chart listing all applicable lessons for each standard. Library Media Specialists can educate students to be evaluative and productive users of any information, whatever its source. What's usually lacking is time to collaboratively develop with teachers the details of the instructional process. If that process isn't developed, it is likely the usual roles will be played: teacher assigns, LMS locates, and no one is really teaching.

These lessons can be used as a package or as a resource to be adapted as needed. They are intended to support, guide, and encourage creativity by both the teacher and the LMS. They focus on the process of learning rather than dissemination of information. Just as the school library has moved far beyond being a warehouse for books, the guides incorporate an array of information resources: print, electronic, and human.

> The new skills do not supersede the old. They build upon the most important ones we have been teaching all along: searching, synthesizing, analyzing, and communicating information.

As a secondary LMS, you are charged with continuing the process started in the elementary school. Most students will come to you with a "basic level" of proficiency in information literacy, as this term is used in *Information Power II*. The progression from "basic" to "proficient" to "exemplary" allows each standard's indicator of competency to be designed for students at their own level. These instructional guides concentrate on leading students from the basic to the proficient level. Exemplary level activities are included where appropriate and suited to a particular curricular area.

While this is a wonderfully exciting time to be a LMS, it also can be intimidating. The reality of the information age can make you feel as if you need to launch a whole new career and learn a whole new set of skills. It may also seem that the comfort of the known, traditional print era must be abandoned or you will become obsolete and unnecessary.

The new skills do not supersede the old. They build upon the most important ones we have been teaching all along: searching, synthesizing, analyzing, and communicating information. It's the resources and tools for access that have changed so dramatically and quickly. Remember, they have changed for teachers also. They are at a loss as much as (or more than) you. The new proficiency standards in information literacy, together with the current best practices for meeting new standards in key curricular areas, offer today's library media specialists an unprecedented opportunity for collaboration and mutual cooperation with other educators.

We've said it before and we're saying it again: it is the unique privilege and responsibility of Library Media Specialists to make sure our students are informationally competent adults. We are indeed giving them Skills for Life.

Christine Allen

Endnote:
1 American Association of School Librarians, and the Association for Educational Communications and Technology. *Information Power: Building Partnerships for Learning.* American Library Association and the Association for Educational Communications and Technology: Chicago, 1998.

Information Literacy Standards for Student Learning

INFORMATION LITERACY

STANDARD 1: The student who is information literate accesses information efficiently and effectively.

STANDARD 2: The student who is information literate evaluates information critically and competently.

STANDARD 3: The student who is information literate uses information accurately and creatively.

INDEPENDENT LEARNING

STANDARD 4: The student who is an independent learner is information literate and pursues information related to personal interests.

STANDARD 5: The student who is an independent learner is information literate and appreciates literature and other creative expressions of information.

STANDARD 6: The student who is an independent learner is information literate and strives for excellence in information seeking and knowledge generation.

SOCIAL RESPONSIBILITY

STANDARD 7: The student who contributes positively to the learning community and to society is information literate and recognizes the importance of information to a democratic society.

STANDARD 8: The student who contributes positively to the learning community and to society is information literate and practices ethical behavior in regard to information and information technology.

STANDARD 9: The student who contributes positively to the learning community and to society is information literate and participates effectively in groups to pursue and generate information.

* See *Information Power: Building Partnerships for Learning* for Indicators and their definitions.

Source: American Association of School Librarians, and the Association for Educational Communications and Technology. Information Power: Building Partnerships for Learning. *American Library Association and the Association for Educational Communications and Technology: Chicago, 1998.*

CORRELATION CHART

	ART	CAREER EDUCATION	CIVICS	EARTH SCIENCE	ENGLISH	FINE ARTS
STANDARD 1						
Indicator 1		Guide 16 (pg. 84)	Guide 13 (pg. 75)			
Indicator 2		Guide 16 (pg. 84)				
Indicator 3		Guide 16 (pg. 84)				
Indicator 4		Guide 16 (pg. 84)				
Indicator 5			Guide 13 (pg. 75)			
STANDARD 2						
Indicator 1						
Indicator 2						
Indicator 3						
Indicator 4		Guide 16 (pg. 84)				
STANDARD 3						
Indicator 1		Guide 16 (pg. 84)	Guide 13 (pg. 75)		Guide 14 (pg. 79)	
Indicator 2		Guide 16 (pg. 84)	Guide 13 (pg. 75)		Guide 14 (pg. 79)	
Indicator 3		Guide 16 (pg. 84)		Guide 38 (pg. 223)	Guide 14 (pg. 79)	
Indicator 4		Guide 16 (pg. 84)		Guide 38 (pg. 223)	Guide 14 (pg. 79)	
STANDARD 4						
Indicator 1						Guide 19 (pg. 108)
Indicator 2						Guide 19 (pg. 108)
STANDARD 5						
Indicator 1						
Indicator 2						
Indicator 3	Guide 35 (pg. 199)					
STANDARD 6						
Indicator 1						
Indicator 2						
STANDARD 7						
Indicator 1	Guide 35 (pg. 199)					
Indicator 2						
STANDARD 8						
Indicator 1						
Indicator 2	Guide 35 (pg. 199)					Guide 19 (pg. 108)
Indicator 3						Guide 19 (pg. 108)
STANDARD 9						
Indicator 1				Guide 38 (pg. 223)		Guide 19 (pg. 108)
Indicator 2				Guide 38 (pg. 223)		Guide 19 (pg. 108)
Indicator 3				Guide 38 (pg. 223)		Guide 19 (pg. 108)
Indicator 4				Guide 38 (pg. 223)		Guide 19 (pg. 108)

CORRELATION CHART cont.

	GEOGRAPHY	HEALTH	HISTORY	INFORMATION SKILLS	LANGUAGE ARTS	LIFE SKILLS
STANDARD 1						
Indicator 1				Guide 1 (pg. 16)		Guide 34 (pg. 189)
Indicator 2				Guide 1 (pg. 16) Guide 8 (pg. 51)		Guide 34 (pg. 189)
Indicator 3	Guide 21 (pg. 115)			Guide 1 (pg. 16)		
Indicator 4	Guide 21 (pg. 115)			Guide 1 (pg. 16) Guide 8 (pg. 51) Guide 9 (pg. 55)	Guide 2 (pg. 23) Guide 5 (pg. 39) Guide 24 (pg. 129)	Guide 34 (pg. 189)
Indicator 5	Guide 21 (pg. 115)			Guide 1 (pg. 16) Guide 3 (pg. 28) Guide 7 (pg. 48) Guide 8 (pg. 51) Guide 9 (pg. 55)	Guide 2 (pg. 23) Guide 5 (pg. 39)	Guide 34 (pg. 189)
STANDARD 2						
Indicator 1	Guide 21 (pg. 115)	Guide 32 (pg. 178) Guide 39 (pg. 226)	Guide 25 (pg. 133)	Guide 1 (pg. 16) Guide 7 (pg. 48) Guide 8 (pg. 51) Guide 9 (pg. 55)	Guide 2 (pg. 23)	Guide 34 (pg. 189)
Indicator 2	Guide 21 (pg. 115)	Guide 32 (pg. 178)	Guide 25 (pg. 133)	Guide 7 (pg. 48) Guide 8 (pg. 51) Guide 9 (pg. 55)		Guide 34 (pg. 189)
Indicator 3	Guide 21 (pg. 115)	Guide 32 (pg. 178)	Guide 25 (pg. 133)	Guide 7 (pg. 48) Guide 8 (pg. 51) Guide 9 (pg. 55)		Guide 34 (pg. 189)
Indicator 4	Guide 21 (pg. 115)	Guide 32 (pg. 178) Guide 39 (pg. 226)	Guide 25 (pg. 133)	Guide 3 (pg. 28) Guide 9 (pg. 55)	Guide 2 (pg. 23) Guide 26 (pg. 140)	Guide 34 (pg. 189)
STANDARD 3						
Indicator 1	Guide 30 (pg. 164)	Guide 39 (pg. 226)		Guide 1 (pg. 16) Guide 3 (pg. 28) Guide 12 (pg. 72) Guide 15 (pg. 82)	Guide 2 (pg. 23) Guide 5 (pg. 39) Guide 26 (pg. 140)	
Indicator 2	Guide 30 (pg. 164)			Guide 1 (pg. 16) Guide 8 (pg. 51)		
Indicator 3				Guide 8 (pg. 51) Guide 12 (pg. 72)	Guide 2 (pg. 23)	
Indicator 4		Guide 39 (pg. 226)	Guide 25 (pg. 133)	Guide 15 (pg. 82)	Guide 2 (pg. 23) Guide 5 (pg. 39) Guide 24 (pg. 129) Guide 26 (pg. 140)	
STANDARD 4						
Indicator 1		Guide 32 (pg. 178)				
Indicator 2	Guide 21 (pg. 115)	Guide 32 (pg. 178)		Guide 15 (pg. 82)		
STANDARD 5						
Indicator 1					Guide 22 (pg. 122) Guide 24 (pg. 129)	
Indicator 2			Guide 25 (pg. 133)		Guide 23 (pg. 125) Guide 24 (pg. 129) Guide 26 (pg. 140)	
Indicator 3			Guide 25 (pg. 133)		Guide 24 (pg. 129) Guide 26 (pg. 140)	
STANDARD 6						
Indicator 1					Guide 29 (pg. 155)	
Indicator 2					Guide 29 (pg. 155)	

CORRELATION CHART cont.

	GEOGRAPHY	HEALTH	HISTORY	INFORMATION SKILLS	LANGUAGE ARTS	LIFE SKILLS
STANDARD 7						
Indicator 1	Guide 30 (pg. 164)	Guide 32 (pg. 178)			Guide 29 (pg. 155)	
Indicator 2					Guide 29 (pg. 155)	
STANDARD 8						
Indicator 1						Guide 34 (pg. 189)
Indicator 2						
Indicator 3						Guide 34 (pg. 189)
STANDARD 9						
Indicator 1		Guide 39 (pg. 226)			Guide 22 (pg. 122) Guide 29 (pg. 155)	
Indicator 2		Guide 39 (pg. 226)			Guide 22 (pg. 122) Guide 29 (pg. 155)	
Indicator 3		Guide 39 (pg. 226)			Guide 22 (pg. 122) Guide 29 (pg. 155)	
Indicator 4		Guide 39 (pg. 226)			Guide 22 (pg. 122) Guide 29 (pg. 155)	

CORRELATION CHART cont.

	LITERATURE	MATHEMATICS	PHYSICS	SCIENCE	SOCIAL STUDIES	U.S. HISTORY
STANDARD 1						
Indicator 1	Guide 6 (pg. 42)				Guide 4 (pg. 34)	Guide 28 (pg. 149)
Indicator 2					Guide 4 (pg. 34) Guide 10 (pg. 61)	
Indicator 3					Guide 4 (pg. 34)	Guide 28 (pg. 149)
Indicator 4	Guide 6 (pg. 42)				Guide 4 (pg. 34) Guide 10 (pg. 61) Guide 18 (pg. 102)	
Indicator 5	Guide 6 (pg. 42)				Guide 4 (pg. 34) Guide 10 (pg. 61)	Guide 11 (pg. 63) Guide 28 (pg. 149)
STANDARD 2						
Indicator 1				Guide 20 (pg. 110) Guide 33 (pg. 184)	Guide 10 (pg. 61)	Guide 36 (pg. 208)
Indicator 2				Guide 20 (pg. 110)	Guide 10 (pg. 61)	Guide 36 (pg. 208)
Indicator 3				Guide 20 (pg. 110) Guide 33 (pg. 184)	Guide 4 (pg. 34) Guide 10 (pg. 61)	
Indicator 4	Guide 6 (pg. 42)		Guide 17 (pg. 95)	Guide 20 (pg. 110) Guide 33 (pg. 184)	Guide 4 (pg. 34) Guide 10 (pg. 61)	Guide 11 (pg. 63) Guide 36 (pg. 208)
STANDARD 3						
Indicator 1	Guide 6 (pg. 42)	Guide 37 (pg. 218)	Guide 17 (pg. 95)	Guide 33 (pg. 184)	Guide 4 (pg. 34) Guide 10 (pg. 61) Guide 18 (pg. 102) Guide 31 (pg. 166) Guide 40 (pg. 229)	Guide 28 (pg. 149) Guide 36 (pg. 208)
Indicator 2	Guide 6 (pg. 42)				Guide 4 (pg. 34)	Guide 36 (pg. 208)
Indicator 3					Guide 4 (pg. 34) Guide 40 (pg. 229)	Guide 28 (pg. 149) Guide 36 (pg. 208)
Indicator 4	Guide 6 (pg. 42)	Guide 37 (pg. 218)	Guide 17 (pg. 95)	Guide 33 (pg. 184)	Guide 10 (pg. 61) Guide 18 (pg. 102) Guide 31 (pg. 166) Guide 40 (pg. 229)	Guide 11 (pg. 63) Guide 28 (pg. 149) Guide 36 (pg. 208)
STANDARD 4						
Indicator 1				Guide 20 (pg. 110)	Guide 18 (pg. 102) Guide 27 (pg. 146)	
Indicator 2						
STANDARD 5						
Indicator 1						
Indicator 2			Guide 17 (pg. 95)			
Indicator 3			Guide 17 (pg. 95)		Guide 40 (pg. 229)	
STANDARD 6						
Indicator 1					Guide 27 (pg. 146)	Guide 28 (pg. 149)
Indicator 2					Guide 31 (pg. 166)	Guide 28 (pg. 149)
STANDARD 7						
Indicator 1					Guide 31 (pg. 166)	
Indicator 2						

SKILLS FOR LIFE: INFORMATION LITERACY FOR GRADES 7-12 9 INTRODUCTION

CORRELATION CHART cont.

	LITERATURE	MATHEMATICS	PHYSICS	SCIENCE	SOCIAL STUDIES	U.S. HISTORY
STANDARD 8						
Indicator 1				Guide 20 (pg. 110)		
Indicator 2				Guide 33 (pg. 184)		
Indicator 3				Guide 20 (pg. 110) Guide 33 (pg. 184)		Guide 36 (pg. 208)
STANDARD 9						
Indicator 1		Guide 37 (pg. 218)			Guide 40 (pg. 229)	
Indicator 2		Guide 37 (pg. 218)				
Indicator 3		Guide 37 (pg. 218)			Guide 40 (pg. 229)	
Indicator 4		Guide 37 (pg. 218)			Guide 40 (pg. 229)	

Information Literacy

CHAPTER 1

Extending Information Literacy Basics

By Mary Alice Anderson

STANDARD 1: The student who is information literate accesses information efficiently and effectively.

Information access has always been a prime purpose of school library media centers. Helping students find information appropriate to their information needs, whether it is for a school assignment or personal interest, has always been a central role for school library media specialists. *Information Power* and the accompanying Information Literacy Standards for Student Learning establish information access as just one part of the entire process of becoming an information literate learner and citizen. But it is the crucial first step since student mastery at this level is critical to further continuation and success.

Today's school library media centers are rapidly changing, information-rich environ-ments. Where we access information is chang-ing as networks and the Internet bring information to classrooms and labs, making it possible for the whole school to become a media center. Defining the information need, formulating questions, selecting the most appropriate resource, and developing search strategies are more important than ever. From using the World Wide Web Virtual Library to locating information about cattle breeds, through designing a coat of arms, the lesson ideas included in this chapter provide many strategies for extending and reinforcing infor-mation literacy basics.

Standard 1 includes five indicators, with additional details provided for basic, profi-cient, and exemplary levels of proficiency. As you read through the five indicators, you will see many similarities to process-based approaches to research, such as the Big6 Skills or Carol Kuhlthau's model. Some of the authors of the lessons in this section of the book refer to these models as key frameworks in developing information literacy school-wide.

Indicators 1 and 2 present the most basic concepts of information literacy. Indicator 1 states that the student "Recognizes the need for information" (*Information Power*, p. 9), and Indicator 2 says that the student "Recognizes that accurate and comprehensive information is the basis for intelligent decision making" (*Information Power*, p. 10). Demonstrated proficiency in these two areas would be crucial to lifelong learning. Indicator 1 emphasizes the importance of recognizing the need for information "beyond one's own knowledge" (*Information Power*, p. 9).

Indicator 2 extends this important concept, asking students to begin to assess the adequacy of the information they are using to make decisions. In "Let's Reinvent the Wheel—Library Orientation," Dianne Sheetz provides a hands-on, active learning approach to library orientation. As students explore information resources at a series of library media stations, they will develop an understanding of how those resources can be used to meet different information needs. This lesson shows how creative media specialists can take a familiar activity (library orientation) and make it more meaningful to the students by adding an information literacy focus with ties to the school curriculum.

The student who "Formulates questions based on information needs" demonstrates an understanding of the concepts related to

> **...It is important to help students use multiple resources and multiple formats. Everyone can help students learn that sometimes a book is a better resource than the Internet.**

Indicator 3. Activities related to this are often an important part of instruction in the research process. For example, at the basic level, students should be able to develop "at least one broad question that will help in finding needed information" (*Information Power*, p. 10). Instead of giving students worksheets to introduce them to research tools such as encyclopedias, almanacs, or informational web sites, students might be asked to work in small groups to develop their own questions. At the proficient level, students reflect on the information they have gathered and assess whether or not it was accurate and complete. Finally, at the exemplary level students would actually assess decisions that they had made to see if the quality of information used in the decision-making process led to making a better decision. At any level, Indicator 3 requires students to develop a reflective, thoughtful approach to information use.

Indicator 4, "Identifies a variety of potential sources of information," is one area that has been greatly impacted by the presence of new technologies in the media center. With more information in all formats available, it is important to help students use multiple resources and multiple formats. Everyone can help students learn that sometimes a book is a better resource than the Internet. At the same time, even basic proficiency in this indicator suggests that the student "lists several sources of information and explains the kind of information found in each" (*Information Power*, p. 11).

The standards also note the importance of human information resources in meeting information needs, in addition to identifying print, nonprint, and electronic resources. To help students meet this standard, media specialists will have to work closely with teachers to ensure that teachers are aware of the range of information resources available today. In addition to the wealth of potential information resources found on the World Wide Web and the Internet, publishers continue to produce more and more excellent print reference materials.

Students who demonstrate exemplary proficiency for Indicator 4 regularly use "a full range of information resources to meet differing information needs" (*Information Power*, p. 11). Deb Logan suggests that students explore a wide range of resources as they complete a "Civil Rights/African American Biography Timeline." The assessment rubric included with this lesson asks students to evaluate different information resources for accuracy, completeness, and detail. In addition, students are asked to translate what they have learned about these leaders into a symbolic format, creating products other than the traditional research papers.

The final indicator for Standard 1 completes the basic cycle of information use by stating that the student "develops and uses successful strategies for locating information." This indicator goes far beyond traditional library skills taught in isolation. Students in junior and senior high school should certainly be able to "list some ideas for how to identify and find needed information" and "explain and apply a plan to access needed information"

(*Information Power*, p. 11). Junior and senior high school students need many opportunities to explore how technology can assist in this process. Frances Campbell and Wanda Higgins, two media specialists in training, show how constructing and using computer databases can help students develop information literacy skills in their lessons, "Exploring Livestock Using Databases and the WWW Virtual Library" and "Crime and Punishment Around the World." The creative use of information that is located by following a systematic search is highlighted in "Create a Coat of Arms" by Maribeth Carmichael. This lesson also highlights the value of teaching information skills in collaboration with a content area. Carmichael's lesson is a challenging and engaging culmination to a study of the Middle Ages and the legends of King Arthur.

Faced with change and multiple challenges, it is increasingly important to make certain that every student has the opportunity to have access to information and every opportunity to learn how to access it effectively and efficiently. Library media specialists need to reach out and share the information literacy process with teachers. Together we can begin to take important first steps toward developing student information literacy.

Mary Alice Anderson, Media Specialist, Winona (Minnesota) Middle School. Minnesota, Information Power Trainer.

TITLE: *Let's Reinvent the Wheel—Library Orientation*

AUTHOR: Dianne T. Sheetz, Library Media Specialist, Signal Knob Middle School, Strasburg, Virginia

CURRICULUM AREA: Information Skills

CURRICULUM CONNECTIONS: Preparation for research in any subject

GRADE LEVELS: 6–8

PREREQUISITES: Basic experience with and general knowledge of library media center

INFORMATION LITERACY STANDARDS FOR STUDENT LEARNING:
Standard 1, Indicators 1–5
Standard 2, Indicator 1
Standard 3, Indicators 1–2

OTHER OUTCOMES/STANDARDS:

- Cross-curriculum collaboration will occur with teachers in any subject area.
- Students will be able to demonstrate they can use different centers in the library to find the information they need. After demonstrating proficiency in using the station or area, the student will receive a "part of the wheel."
- When the student has received all parts, he or she will be able to create a wheel identifying specific locations for finding information within the library media center and the relationship between information retrieval and usage.
- Students will develop confidence in knowing how to use the various stations in the library media center, as well as determining which stations are most relevant to their research questions.

MATERIALS:

- Overhead projector and transparencies or computer and projection capabilities
- Chalk or white board
- Pre-made parts of the Library Media Center wheel
- Outline of wheel onto which parts may be glued
- Computers and databases for research

STRATEGIES:

This can be used as an orientation to a new library media center. At various other times throughout the school year, these activities may be used to re-introduce students to resources on research topics in any subject matter for all grade levels.

- Over a six-week period, students come to the library and are shown the different "stations" of available resources. For example, one station would be a computer loaded with an interactive encyclopedia.

■ After a brief (10-minute) overview of the station by the library media specialist, students would begin to use the station and try to find answers to questions prepared collaboratively by the library media specialist and teacher.

■ The cooperating teacher would continue to send students in small groups to work on the stations in the library over the 6-week period until those students felt competent and comfortable with the station. At that time, individual students would ask to be observed and evaluated by the library media specialist, the teacher or another designated adult or aide.

■ Upon successful completion of that station, the student would receive the corresponding "spoke" of the library wheel to be glued to his/her wheel outline, along with the date and signature of the evaluator.

■ When students have been evaluated at all stations, they will have a completed wheel showing the relationship between information resources and the Information Literacy Standards or other curricular goals and objectives.

Several stations may be covered each week if the stations are similar in nature. For example, fiction and nonfiction stacks could be covered in the same instructional period as the card catalog, which gives all students an opportunity to practice their information skills throughout the library without congregating in one specific area. The students may request to be evaluated at any time during the six week period by the designated evaluator.

The following stations can be found in a library media center:

1 Card catalog or online card catalog work stations

2 Reference books (encyclopedia, atlas, dictionary, almanac, thesaurus, etc.)

3 Vertical file

4 Fiction and nonfiction stacks

5 Internet workstations

6 Online database (example: Electric Library) workstations

7 Interactive encyclopedia workstations

8 CD-ROM database (example: Infotrac) workstations

EVALUATION/CRITIQUE:

1 Checklist from students indicating who has evaluated them at a particular station with date, time, and signature of evaluator (could be combined with 2)

2 Wheel outline with completed parts of the wheel attached (library orientation)

3 Completed information skills sheet for class (below)

COMMENTS/TIPS/FOLLOW-UP:

The exciting thing about this activity is that students make a product allowing them to visualize what they have learned. The wheel, when completed, shows a process of finding information to complete lesson assignments and helps students to understand which stations provide the best information for particular research topics. Students feel competent about using all areas of the library media center, and another "prize," such as a special pencil, could be awarded for all those who complete the wheel. The activity could also be ongoing, so students would not be on a time schedule to complete the stations.

Another process that works is to have seventh or eighth grade mentors teach the skill to incoming sixth graders, or to use high achievers to work with lower achievers in any grade level. This method is especially good to use with new students who are not yet familiar with its library media center resources.

Library Media Specialist will fill in specific sources as appropriate

Mathematics (outer circle)
> Interactive Encyclopedia (inner circle)
> Fiction/Non-fiction Books (inner circle)

Science (outer circle)
> Vertical File Materials (inner circle)

English (outer circle)
> Card Catalog or OPAC (inner circle)

Social Studies (outer circle)
> CD-ROM Database (inner circle)

Reading (outer circle)
> Online Database Periodicals (inner circle)

Art (outer circle)
> Internet Sources (inner circle)

History (outer circle)
> Reference Books (inner circle)

Information (place at center of circle)

INFORMATION SKILLS SHEET:

CARD CATALOG (ELECTRONIC)

1 Locate the computerized card catalog station in your library.

2 Go to the search screen and pick a subject in which you are interested.

How many materials are available in your library when you search your subject?

How many of those materials found are fiction?

How many are videotapes?

3 Start a new search and this time look for your favorite author.

How many materials are found in your library written by your favorite author?

Is there a biography about your author?

Write the title and author of the biography.

4 List 5 types of materials found in your library and their call numbers.

(Example: Fiction book, F Pau)

a.

b.

c.

d.

e.

5 Name the three main ways to search for materials in the electronic card catalog.

a.

b.

c.

You have now completed the Electronic Card Catalog center and may go on to the Reference Book center.

INFORMATION SKILLS SHEET:

CARD CATALOG (PHYSICAL)

1 Locate the card catalog in your library.

How many materials are found when you look up the word *bird*?

How many of those materials found are books?

Did you find any magazines about birds? If so, what is the title of the magazine?

2 Now search for your favorite author.

How many materials are found in your library written by your favorite author?

How many of those books are Fiction?

Is there a biography about your author?

Write the title and author of the biography.

3 Name 5 types of materials found in your library and their call numbers.

(Example: Fiction book, F Pau)

a.

b.

c.

d.

e.

4 Name the three main types of cards used to organize materials in the card catalog.

a.

b.

c.

You have now completed the Card Catalog center and may go on to the Reference Book center.

STUDENT CHECKLIST:

Student name:_____ Grade:_____

Teacher:_____

STATION COMPLETED	DATE	TIME	AUTHORIZED SIGNATURE
1. Card Catalog			
2 Reference Books			
3 Vertical File			
4 Fiction/Nonfiction			
5 Internet			
6 Online Database			
7 Interactive Encyclopedia			
8 CD-ROM Database			

When you have completed all the stations on this sheet and have received the appropriate signatures, you are finished with the Library Media Center orientation. Take this completed sheet to your Library Media Specialist for your final puzzle pieces to complete your "wheel."

Congratulations! You have now mastered the skills to make you an effective user of the information in your Library Media Center.

TITLE: *Civil Rights/African American Biography Time Line*

AUTHOR: Debra Kay Logan, Library Media Specialist, Taft Middle School, Marion, Ohio

CURRICULUM AREA: Language Arts

CURRICULUM CONNECTIONS: Social Studies

GRADE LEVEL: 7

PREREQUISITES: Topic skills, Dewey and electronic search strategies

INFORMATION LITERACY STANDARDS FOR STUDENT LEARNING
Standard 1, Indicators 4, 5
Standard 2, Indicators 1, 4
Standard 3, Indicators 1, 3, 4

MATERIALS/SOURCES NEEDED:
■ Biography Time Line note-taking sheet
■ Biography Time Line Project check sheet
■ Computer workstations
■ Books, magazines, globe(s)
■ Overhead or white/chalk board
■ CD-ROM resources and Internet access
■ Unlined paper or 5x8 note cards and markers or colored pencils

STRATEGIES:
■ Students will analyze and summarize information they have gathered about famous African Americans and civil rights leaders.
■ Each student will then design and create a symbol to represent a famous individual.
■ After information and symbols are shared with the class, the symbols will be posted in chronological order on a bulletin board to create a timeline of African American or civil rights history.
■ In language arts class, this information can be related to class discussions about the class novel, such as *Roll of Thunder Hear My Cry* by Mildred Taylor.

Some researchable famous African Americans include:

Hank Aaron, Muhammad Ali, Marian Anderson, Maya Angelou, Louis Armstrong, Arthur Ashe, Crispus Attucks, James Baldwin, Benjamin Banneker, James Pierson Beckwourth, Mary McLeod Bethune, Ron Brown, Ralph Bunche, George Washington Carver, Shirley Chisholm, Bessie Coleman, Bill Cosby, Paul Cuffe, Benjamin O. Davis, Sr., Benjamin O. Davis, Jr., Frederick Douglass, Charles

R. Drew, W.E.B. DuBois, Paul Laurence Dunbar, Duke Ellington, Medgar Evers, Marcus Mosiah Garvey, Alex Haley, Virginia Hamilton, W. C. Handy, Matthew Henson, Langston Hughes, Bo Jackson, Rev. Jesse Jackson, Frederick McKinley Jones, Quincy Jones, Scott Joplin, Barbara Jordan, Michael Jordan, Jackie Joyner-Kersee, Percy L. Julian, Rev. Martin Luther King Jr., Lewis Howard Latimer, Spike Lee, Joe Louis, Thurgood Marshall, Elijah McCoy, Hattie McDaniel, Thelonius Monk, Garrett A. Morgan, Toni Morrison, Jesse Owens, Rosa Parks, Sidney Poitier, Colin Powell, Asa Philip Randolph, Norbert Rillieux, Jackie Robinson, Wilma Rudolph, Barry Sanders, Dred Scott, Emmitt Smith, Clarence Thomas, Frank Thomas, Sojourner Truth, Harriet Tubman, Nat Turner, Madame C. J. Walker, Maggie Lena Walker, Booker T. Washington, Phyllis Wheatley, Dr. Daniel Hale Williams, Dave Winfield, Oprah Winfrey, Granville Woods, Dr. Carter G. Woodson, and Malcolm X

Although this is not a comprehensive list, it includes African Americans who have made a wide variety of contributions to American history and culture. To emphasize civil rights, in addition to selecting names from the above list, consider including international figures such as: Nelson Mandela and Archbishop Desmond Tutu. To expand the civil rights topic further, add people like César Chávez (not an African American, but a civil rights leader).

STEPS:

1 Share idea of creating a time line with students. Discuss possible ways people could be represented. Show examples from other time lines (in print resources).

2 Tell students they will be researching two individuals and selecting one to be represented in the time line. They will also be telling the class about their person and explaining how the symbol represents him/her.

3 Discuss project evaluation with students. Have the Biography Time Line Project Check Sheet available. Note: Two Biography Time Line Project sheets will fit on a single piece of paper.

4 Review note-taking sheet with students, emphasizing that it is just a note-taking sheet. Information should not be in complete sentences and should not be copied. Clarify any new vocabulary. Use overhead or white/chalk board to show the ways that birth and death dates are represented in reference works. For example:

```
(1823-1912)
b. 1823 d.1912
m.1840
(1947-  )
c. 1823
```

■ First, post the dates in parentheses and ask the group what that means. Then show the *b.* and *d.* abbreviations and ask what they represent. Talk about missing death dates and what they mean. (I like to ask them not to kill anyone off in order to fill in a blank). This is another good opportunity to remind students they do not have to fill in all the blanks on note-taking sheets. Also, if there is no death date, remind them to check the date of their source. If a source is more than three years old, students should check death dates in a newer resource.

■ Throw in the *m.* abbreviation and ask students to guess what the *m* means. Usually, at least one student will figure out what it represents.

- Finally, introduce *circa* or *c* and what it means. I start by asking my students, "Over a hundred years ago would people have gotten a new calendar every year?" Then we talk about if you would have always known the day's date. We also talk about how records can be lost and destroyed. In other words, describe how sometimes the best we can do now, given the facts we have, is "about" or "circa" regarding past situations in general.

- Having discussed what information is needed and how it is to be used, the next step is to explore possible research resources. Begin by asking whether extensive information or brief facts will be needed. When they say brief facts, ask what type of resource you would use as a last resort. (They should say a biography.)

- Then have students predict possible resources. As they mention different types of resources, talk about how each is used. Review things like using quotation marks or hyphens when searching a name online. I find I always need to remind students to look up biographical information using a person's last name in print resources. When discussing encyclopedias (print, CD-ROM, and online), remind students they are a great place to start if you don't know anything about the person you are researching as they give you the basics, as well as other topics to search.

- When students are through suggesting possible resources, note ones they may have missed. This is usually the best time to share biographical dictionaries and collective biographies. Remind students once they have identified their person's field of endeavor, they can also search under topics related to that field.

- Assist students as they work. Watch for copying and help individual students with note-taking problems.

- As students are finishing their research, have them begin work on the person's symbol. Remind students that their symbol papers need to include the person's name, birth date, and death date.

WRAP-UP:

Students share with the class why they have created their particular symbol to represent the person researched. The symbols are then arranged by date and displayed. Since this project is usually done by several classes, any duplicates are placed under the first symbol representing a particular person.

EVALUATION: Use the Biography Time Line Project Check Sheet to evaluate projects.

BIOGRAPHY TIME LINE PROJECT CHECK SHEET

Names: _____

_____

	NOT YET! ☹	SOMETIMES 😐	OFTEN ☺	YES! ☺
The project is full of information which is accurate, clear, complete, and detailed.				
Followed directions and used time well.				
Art: The symbol is well planned, colorful, neat and original.				
Presentation: The presentation was loud enough, easy to hear, and made good use of visual aids.				
Comments/Tips/Follow-up:				

Two research days are sufficient for this project. Allow an additional day for work on the symbol. (The symbol can be done in class or at home.) Presentations only take one day. If done the last week of January, the timeline can be on display during Black History Month in February.

1 This can be an individual or collaborative project. For a collaborative project, organize students in groups of three. Assign people to be researched by printing their names on note-taking sheets prior to distribution. Make sure each group researches an array of individuals. (Be sure to include historic people, civil rights leaders, athletes, writers and entertainers). When students finish, discuss the people researched within the small group. As a group, students decide which three people to feature with their time line symbols. The artwork, lettering, and presentation are thus group efforts.

2 Another option would be to have students use a program like Print Shop, PrintMaster, or Microsoft Publisher to create an illustrated sign with the person's name, life span, and a clip-art symbol. To do this, use a multimedia projector or LCD panel to demonstrate the use of a desktop publishing program. Show how to:

■ Create a new sign-type document.

■ Add text to the document.

■ Change text style and size.

■ Select and add graphics to a document.

■ Saving a document.

Always be prepared to assist students as they work.

BIOGRAPHY NOTE-TAKING SHEET:

Name:_____

BIOGRAPHY TIME LINE PROJECT

Name: _____

Date of Birth:_____

Date of Death:_____

Education (if any)_____
_____

Accomplishment (why famous)_____
_____
_____
_____
_____

Awards (if any):_____

Interesting facts:_____
_____
_____
_____
_____
_____

TITLE: *Exploring Databases Using Livestock and the WWW Virtual Library*

AUTHOR: Frances Campbell, Graduate Student, James Madison University, Harrisonburg, Virginia

CURRICULUM AREA: Information Skills

CURRICULUM CONNECTIONS: Agricultural Education, Vocational Education

GRADE LEVELS: 7–8

PREREQUISITES: Basic computer and Internet experience. Basic understanding and use of a database. See other database adaptations with comments/tips/follow-ups at end of lesson.

INFORMATION LITERACY STANDARDS FOR STUDENT LEARNING:
Standard 1, Indicator 5
Standard 2, Indicator 4
Standard 3, Indicator 1

MATERIALS/SOURCES NEEDED:
- Black or whiteboard
- Overhead/Transparencies
- Computer with ability to project for whole class viewing
- Activity Sheet 1 – reproducible
- Activity Sheet 2 – reproducible
- Internet Access

STRATEGIES:
- Library media specialist, Agriculture teacher, and students create an Agricultural/Livestock database on the board or overhead.
- Students use created database (Activity Sheet 1) as a reference guide to complete Livestock Type/Breed Work Sheet (Activity Sheet 2) using the WWW Virtual Library database.
- The teacher and the library media specialist should collaboratively decide who will introduce students to the various steps included in this activity.

STEPS:

1 Library media specialist briefly explains that a database is a "supermarket" collection of information. Use a grocery store as an example. Ask students how products are arranged. For example, fruit and produce are in one section, cereal is in another section, and laundry detergent and cleaning products are in a different section. In the laundry section, detergents are separated by brand name and further subdivided as powder or liquid detergent. These divisions would represent subfields within a larger field. Ask students why products are arranged this way. How does this arrangement help them to locate items? Explain that databases do the same thing, only with information.

2 Using board or overhead, the library media specialist titles the database "Agriculture." The library media specialist explains that Agriculture has many facets, but right now students will explore Mammal Livestock Types and Breeds. The library media specialist adds Livestock (Mammals) to the database. A sample of a partial Livestock Database can be found at the end of the lesson. The library media specialist could change entries to represent breeds familiar to students or common to the region.

3 The library media specialist asks students to identify the two major types of cattle and explain the importance of each. The library media specialist adds *Beef* and *Dairy* fields to the database. The library media specialist asks students to identify major breeds of beef cattle and adds *Beef Breeds* to the database. The library media specialist asks students to identify the major breeds of dairy cattle and adds *Dairy Breeds* to database. Point out to students how they are building a database.

4 Provide copies of Activity Sheet 1 (partially completed Cattle Database) for students. Point out that breeds are listed in alphabetical order. This becomes another sub-field of their database. The library media specialist and students complete Activity Sheet 1 together. The library media specialist asks students for other livestock types and breeds and continues to develop the Livestock Database on the board or overhead as students complete the database section of Activity Sheet 1. Ask students to complete Activity Sheet 1 by explaining in their own words why databases are created and how they work.

5 Upon completion of Activity Sheet 1, students use the database they created as a reference guide for Activity Sheet 2. The library media specialist, using a computer and projector, introduces students to The WWW Virtual Library (**http://www.vlib.org/Home.html**).

6 Using the home page of the Virtual Library, point out the different subject directories. Students will use the **Agriculture** Subject Directory. Click on the main (boldface) **Agriculture** Directory Heading, then click **Livestock**. Under Species Specific Information, click **Beef Cattle**; this brings you to the Beef Cattle Resources page. On the Beef Cattle Resources page, under Breed Information, click **Breeds of Cattle–Oklahoma State**. This database is provided and maintained by the Animal Science Dept. of Oklahoma State University. This is an excellent site to use for completion of Activity Sheet 2. The Breeds of Livestock Home Page Address is **http://www.ansi.okstate.edu/breeds/**. Use of the site is self- explanatory. Agripedia (**http://frost.ca.uky.edu/agripedia/index.htm**) is a similar site. Using the site index or search feature makes it easy for students to locate information about cattle breeds.

7 To complete Activity Sheet 2, students select a Livestock Type and Breed of personal interest. Student then gathers information necessary to complete handout. Student has successfully mastered the assignment when both Activity Sheet 1 and 2 are completed.

8 Have students browse the **AGRICULTURE** Directory of the WWW Virtual Library or the Subject Index of Agripedia to explore other interesting topic areas.

COMMENTS/TIPS/FOLLOW-UP:

Other animals can be used as the subject of this database exploration. Cats, dogs, and poultry are all particularly well-suited because there are so many breeds.

For Cats: Cat Fanciers
(**http://www.fanciers.com/breeds.html**) This site provides an alphabetical listing of cat breeds with information and pictures for each breed.

For Dogs: American Kennel Club
(**http://www.akc.org/bredgrp.htm**) Here you will find 140 some recognized dog breeds with information, pictures and some history for each.

For Poultry: Department of Animal Science—Oklahoma State University
(**http://www.ansi.okstate.edu/poultry**) At this site you pull up pictures and breed information on chicken, geese, ducks, and turkeys.

ACTIVITY SHEET #1

Name: _____

BEEF CATTLE	DAIRY CATTLE					
Angus – Black	Brown Swiss					
Angus – Red	Guernsey					
Brahman	Holstein					
Hereford	Jersey					
Limousin						
Simmental						

Explain in your own words how databases are created and how they work.

_____

_____

_____

_____

_____

_____

_____

_____

LIBRARY MEDIA SPECIALIST/TEACHER GUIDE

AGRICULTURE
LIVESTOCK — MAMMALS

BEEF CATTLE	DAIRY CATTLE	SWINE	SHEEP	GOATS	HORSES	OTHER/ EXOTIC
Angus – Black	Brown Swiss	Berkshire	Cheviot	Alpine	Arabian	Buffalo
Angus – Red	Guernsey	Duroc	Dorset	Angora	Belgian	Camel
Brahman	Holstein	Hampshire	Hampshire	Nubian	PasoFino	Deer
Hereford	Jersey	Landrace	Merino	Toggenburg	Quarter Horse	Elk
Limousin		Poland China	Rambouillet		Saddlebred	Llama
Simmental		Yorkshire	Suffolk		Tenn. Walker	Yak

ACTIVITY SHEET #2

Name: _____

Type of Livestock: _____

Approximate Time and Area of Domestication: _____
_____
_____
_____
_____

Reasons for Domestication: _____
_____
_____
_____
_____

Breed: _____

Country of Primary Use: _____

History of Origin: _____
_____
_____
_____
_____

Characteristics (color, mature height, number of offspring, etc.): _____
_____
_____
_____
_____

Interesting Facts: _____
_____
_____
_____

URL (Citation Address): _____

TITLE: *Crime and Punishment Around the World*

AUTHOR: Wanda P. Higgins, Graduate Student, James Madison University, Harrisonburg, Virginia

CURRICULUM AREA: Social Studies

CURRICULUM CONNECTION: Any subject area

GRADE LEVELS: 9–12

PREREQUISITES: Keyboarding skills, research experience.

INFORMATION LITERACY STANDARDS FOR STUDENT LEARNING:
Standard 1, Indicators 1–5
Standard 2, Indicators 3–4
Standard 3, Indicators 1–3

OTHER OUTCOMES/STANDARDS:

MULTIPLE INTELLIGENCES
Because intelligence involves a set of skills enabling a person to solve problems, and no two students are the same, instructional design based on multiple intelligences is preferred by many teachers and library media specialists. This lesson allows students to use a variety of activities for learning a content area. It involves group work, role playing, and the creation of a database with several extension activities.

OBJECTIVES:
- Students will evaluate and compare the judicial procedures and criminal statistics of the United States with Mexico, Russia, and China.
- Students will use a variety of research resources to locate information.
- Students will create a database of criminal statistics and procedures.
- Students will sort information using a database and be able to explain the terms *record, fields,* and *sort.*

MATERIALS/SOURCES NEEDED:
- Chalk or White board
- Role play of a database (see page 37)
- Computer and ability to project for whole class viewing
- Appropriate video clip scene showing a criminal sentencing
- A computer lab with database management system or enough computers and database software so no more than two students have to share
- Research pathfinder (see page 38)

STRATEGIES:

The Library Media Specialist will:

- Gather reference resources for criminal procedures, criminal statistics and punishments for the United States, Mexico, Russia, and China.
- Develop a research pathfinder to assist students in their search for information resources
- Discuss and review purposes of electronic databases.
- Explain a database management system (DBMS).
- Model a lesson on how to create a database.
- Assist students with the development of their database and data input.

STEPS:

1 View scene from *Gideon's Trumpet* showing Mr. Gideon's sentencing to prison. Discuss the scene and explain to students that different countries have different types of judicial procedures and punishments.

2 Explain that databases are an effective way to organize information and to make comparisons.

3 Have students participate in a role play of a database. Students are given cards with selected information on it and must organize themselves according to the information. Ask students a series of questions to demonstrate the terms *record, field,* and *sort.* (See Role-Play for a database.)

4 In groups, have students brainstorm a list of fields that might be found in a database on crimes, punishments, and judicial procedures. Have each group of students share their list with the class. Students will take notes from the list developed by each group.

5 Use a computer connected to a monitor (with the ability to project for whole-class viewing). While students are at computer stations, guide students through the database management system.

6 After modeling one database, give students a list of fields and have them independently create a database. Monitor students' progress and assist students who need help.

7 Review key procedures for creating a database and introduce the research pathfinder.

8 Discuss with students the many databases available in the media center: card catalog, Internet, and CD-ROM encyclopedias.

WRAP-UP:

- Remind students that the pathfinder will help them locate their information.
- Explain to students that they will create an effective way to organize information in their database.
- Using this information, students can make comparisons between countries.

EVALUATION/CRITIQUE:

- Check and review students' pathfinders to monitor progress on their research.
- Have students explain to a partner why their database is organized the way it is and how it might be used in class.
- Evaluate students' databases for accurate information.

COMMENTS/TIPS/FOLLOW-UP:

■ Students enjoy this lesson because of the variety of activities. Once students have gathered all of their data, review the steps for creating a database. Students can work in groups if there is a lack of computers or if you have slower students who may need assistance. Students who can produce a database will be able to use this skill later in a variety of classes.

■ An extension of this lesson is to have students create products in multiple formats using the information from their databases, such as posters, graphs, charts, and brochures that can be displayed in the media center.

■ The databases students created can be saved and updated each year by a new class.

■ The selection of countries for this lesson was based on an Advance Placement Comparative Government course. You may want to use other countries of the world or, reduce the number from five to three. Embassies are a good source of information.

ROLE PLAY FOR A DATABASE

You may use any source of information for your role play, such as automobiles, sport statistics, telephone books, or movies. Whatever interests students will work.

STEP ONE:: Write your fields on index cards. For example:

Field: Movies	Field: Genre	Field: Rating
Superman	Action	PG
Gone With the Wind	Classic	PG
Shakespeare in Love	Drama	R
A Bug's Life	Family	G

Make sure you have an index card for each member of the class.

STEP TWO: Have students form groups according to the information on their index cards. Explain that each group represents a field.

STEP THREE: Have one student perform a search. Search for a movie (any movie). This search should include genre and rating. Three students will form a group. Explain to the class that this group of students forms a record.

STEPFOUR: Have another student perform a search. Search for all PG movies. This search will include all PG movies, their genres, and their titles. These students will form a group. Explain to the class that this group of students forms a record. This demonstrates another way to search a database and to locate information.

STEP FIVE: Instruct students to sort themselves by alphabetical order, ratings, or other criteria. Explain that this is how the sort function in a database performs.

STEP SIX: Summarize the lesson and review the key terms of *field, record,* and *sort.*

PATHFINDER FOR A DATABASE

Use this Pathfinder for your research and record your information on your own paper. Before you start searching:

1 **WHAT ARE YOU LOOKING FOR?** Check your list against the list created in class.

Here is a start:

assaults	rape	drug possession
car thefts	kidnapping	people in prison
number of guns	capital punishment	Judicial Review
murder	robberies	Supreme Court
Appeals Court	jury trial	lawyers
witnesses	battery	larceny
manslaughter	size of police force	

2 **THE COUNTRIES YOU ARE RESEARCHING:**

Mexico   Russia   China   United States

3 **INTERNET SEARCH:**

KEYWORDS about this topic: _____

_____

WHERE YOU WILL SEARCH:

___Alta Vista   ___HotBot   ___Excite   ___Yahoo   ___Other

4 **ENCYCLOPEDIA:** Title One_____

5 **ENCYCLOPEDIA:** Title Two_____

6 **ALMANACS** (Use at least 2)

Title-date_____

Title-date_____

7 **CD-ROM ENCYCLOPEDIA**

Title-date_____

TITLE: *Thematic Film Analysis*

AUTHOR : Lesley S. J. Farmer, Associate Professor, California State University, Long Beach

CURRICULUM AREA: Language arts

CURRICULUM CONNECTION: Social Studies (or content analysis for any subject involving visuals)

GRADE LEVELS: 9–12

PREREQUISITE: Basic media literacy experience in video editing (optional)

INFORMATION LITERACY STANDARDS FOR STUDENT LEARNING:
Standard 1, Indicators 4, 5
Standard 3, Indicators 1, 4

LEARNING EXPECTATIONS/OUTCOMES:

BIG6: Task Definition/Identify information needed:
- Students will be able to identify information needed to identify videos thematically and find information within the source.
- Students will be able to locate video sources about a theme.
- Students will be able to locate relevant scenes about a theme.

Use of Information/Extract relevant information:

- Students will be able to determine which scenes best exemplify a theme.

Synthesis/Organize information from multiple source and present the information:
- Students will be able to sequence video clips logically.
- Students will be able to edit video images.
- Students will be able to create commentary on film treatments.

MATERIALS/SOURCES NEEDED:
- Sources on video themes
- Videotapes
- Video editing equipment (at least TV/VCR)

STRATEGIES:

1 Library media specialist will discuss themes found in movies: love, duty, betrayal, family relationships.

2 Library media specialist will discuss ways that movies communicate an attitude about a theme; for instance how can one tell if a movie is pro-war or anti-war?

3 Library media specialist will discuss media literacy elements that "cue" the viewer, such as music, costume, lighting, camera angle, use of space, and dialogue.

4 Library media specialist will formally define content analysis and link it to media literacy.

5 Library media specialist or content teacher will discuss film commentary, giving exemplars.

STEPS:

1 Students choose a theme. They may want to work in pairs.

2 Students locate videos that treat that theme.

3 Students select key video scenes/clips that best exemplify the theme.

4 Students sequence the video clips logically to develop their theme.

5 Students create commentary to accompany the video clips.

6 Students produce a video of video clips following copyright guidelines.

7 Students present their video to class with commentary.

WRAP-UP:

Students compare video treatments of themes in terms of content and media. Library media specialist explains how content analysis methods transfer to different media.

EVALUATION/CRITIQUE:

1 Students evaluate peer videos in terms of relevance and choice of clips.

2 Students evaluate peer commentary in terms of persuasiveness, media literacy knowledge, thoroughness, and insight.

COMMENTS/TIPS/FOLLOW-UP:

■ To help students understand the concept of visual content analysis, show sections of a video such as "Romeo and Juliet." Have them focus on images or scenes that deal with conflict. Guiding questions might be: "How does the filmmaker show you that the two families are rivals?" "How can you tell that Romeo and Juliet are in conflict with their parents?" "What are the visual cues?" "What are the sound cues?"

■ Ask them to identify key scenes ("If you had only one minute, what would you choose, and why?"). Students should also be reminded to choose a clip that is long enough (at least 30 seconds) to build a strong case for their chosen theme.

■ To guide students in sequencing video clips, you might show them a section of the video "That's Entertainment" or have students recall past Oscar shows and the thematic video clips.

■ If video editing equipment is not available (and/or students don't have the time to learn how to edit), they can do pseudo-editing with two TV/VCR stations cabled together or one TV/VCR station cabled to a camcorder. They need to pre-set each video to the start of the desired clip (usually a couple of seconds before the scene). The master tape (on which they will record the clip) is in one VCR or camcorder on "record, pause." When the player VCR begins the clip, the student hits the record/play button. At the end of the clip, the student hits the pause button again. The same process is repeated for each clip.

- If only one TV/VCR station is available, students can create their presentation by giving an oral commentary between videotape set-ups (i.e., introduce the theme and talk about the first clip, insert the video and play it, stop the video and remove the tape, comment on the second clip while changing tapes, etc.) This is a good time to introduce students to the current copyright guidelines addressing the use of video clips in student multimedia productions. Require students to follow the guidelines in their finished products.

- To help students with commentary, you might want them to read film reviews and books on film themes.

- Students can create a voice-over commentary on the videotape if the camcorder has that option (audio only recording). However, the video will then lose the original sound. Students can make a presentation, pausing at each clip to give their commentary, or they can provide a written commentary that the viewer can refer to at any point. Sophisticated video editors can use a title card between clips and voice-over the commentary during the "still" image.

- Students may want to develop criteria for evaluating the relevance and strength of a video clip.

BIBLIOGRAPHY OF ELECTRONIC SOURCES:

Most Internet search engines have movie sections. Here are some good starting points:

Cinemachine: The Movie Review Search Engine
http://www.cinemachine.com/

The Internet Movie Database
http://www.imdb.com/

Internet Public Library Movies Reference
http://www.ipl.org/ref/RR/static/ent5000.html

Lycos Entertainment Guide: Movies
http://www.lycos.com/entertainment/movies/
Select film genres under Web Directory

INSTRUCTIONAL GUIDE 6

TITLE: Create a Coat of Arms

AUTHOR: Maribeth Carmichael, Media Specialist, Sherando High School, Stephens City, Virginia

CURRICULUM AREA: Literature

CURRICULUM CONNECTIONS: Social studies

GRADE LEVEL: 12

PREREQUISITES: Students have studied the historical background of the Middle Ages, read *Le Morte D'Arthur* by Sir Thomas Mallory and portions of *The Canterbury Tales*, and briefly discussed coats of arms.

INFORMATION LITERACY STANDARDS FOR STUDENT LEARNING:
Standard 1, Indicators 1, 4, 5
Standard 2, Indicator 4
Standard 3, Indicators 1, 2, 4

OTHER OUTCOMES/STANDARDS:
BIG6

- Students will study the history of heraldry and the coat of arms. Examples of questions they will attempt to answer are: When and why did heraldry begin? What purpose did the coat of arms serve? What do the colors and symbols on the coat of arms represent? (Task Definition)

- In the library, the library media specialist will brainstorm with the class for possible Internet search strategies. (Information-seeking Strategies)

- With assistance from both the library media specialist and teacher, the students will conduct research in the library. (Location and Access)

- Once they have collected the necessary information, the students will design their own family coat of arms. They will also write a paper explaining why they have chosen to include certain colors and symbols and how they represent their own family. (Use of Information)

- Through use of creative means (either artistic, collage, or computer format), students will create an image of their coat of arms. (Synthesis)

- Upon completion, the library media specialist and classroom teacher will evaluate the student's progress. (Evaluation)

- Students should come away from the project with a basic understanding of Boolean search skill strategies and have experience searching on the Internet.

MATERIALS/SOURCES NEEDED:

- Internet access
- Word processor
- Color printer
- Construction paper, poster board
- Glue, scissors
- Colored pencils, crayons, markers, colored chalk

STRATEGIES:

1 The library media specialist will explain, through a brief lecture, Internet search skills that show the students how to find information concerning the history of heraldry, as well as explaining the basics of Boolean searching.

2 As a class, the students will attempt to determine which search statements will find the best information regarding heraldry and coat of arms. Through brainstorming, the students will compile a list of possible search statements on the board. This list should include terms such as *Crusades, Middle Ages, coat of arms, heraldry, knighthood,* and *family crest.*

3 Once the list is completed, the library media specialist will explain how the word *and* can enhance and change the search.

4 The students will then individually choose the statements they would like to try. They will turn in their top three search statements to the library media specialist before they begin their search.

5 Students will use these statements to begin their research on the Internet. The teacher and library media specialist will work together to assist the students in finding the most useful sites in order to complete the project. Students will note sites, using MLA guidelines (or another format adopted by the school) for bibliographic citations of electronic resources.

6 Upon completing their research, the students will return to class and as a whole group discuss the parts of a coat of arms. During this time, the "class artist" could draw and label a sample coat of arms on the board. This discussion will allow students to share and compare the information they found.

7 The students will then begin work on creating their own family coat of arms and composing their written papers using a word processing program. The coat of arms will be an illustration determined by the student's own individual abilities. The coat of arms could be an illustration, a collage, or poster.

8 Accompanying the coat or arms will be a 1–2 page written paper that explains the features of the student's coat of arms. Students should discuss why they included certain colors and symbols in their coat of arms. This work will be divided between the library media center and the classroom according to students' individual needs.

EVALUATION/CRITIQUE:

Students will be evaluated by both the teacher and the library media specialist using a rubric. The rubric will assess the research trail, the creativity and accuracy of the coat of arms, as well as the written paper (see sample rubric).

SAMPLE GRADING RUBRIC

WRITTEN EXPLANATION OF COAT OF ARMS   35%
- Paper explains the colors and symbols of coat of arms.
- Paper includes a bibliography.
- Paper is well-written (spelling, grammar, proofreading).
- Paper is word-processed.

CREATIVITY/ORIGINALITY OF COAT OF ARMS   30%
- Student creatively and attractively displays coat of arms.

ACCURACY OF COAT OF ARMS, INCLUDING LABELING OF PARTS   25%
- Student labels the various parts of a coat of arms.
- Coat of arms is correct (as per research results).

SEARCH STATEMENT/RESEARCH TRAIL   10%
- Student submits search statements used during research.
- Student remained on task (as observed by Library media specialist and teacher).
- Student's research is reflected in the coat of arms and paper—
  both of which should be factual and accurate.
- Student's research is accurately and completely cited. (as per school guidelines).

TOTAL SCORE   100%

RATIONALE/COMMENTS/TIPS/FOLLOW-UP:

Once the projects have been completed, with the student's permission they will be displayed in the library. There are some good Internet sites which explain the parts of a coat of arms and what the symbols and colors represent. Students who are not artistic but are computer-literate will be able to copy and paste symbols they want to include in their coat of arms to Microsoft Word, print, and create a collage-type coat of arms. Create an example coat of arms using clip art and a simple drawing program.

WEB RESOURCES:

Coats of Arms from Ireland and Around the World
http://homepage.tinet.ie/~donnaweb/

Heraldica
http://www.heraldica.org/intro.htm

Heraldry on the Internet
http://digiserve.com/heraldry/

Le Morte D'Arthur
http://www.frognet.net/~wentwrth/arthur/
Site created by AP British Literature students

CHAPTER 2

Creating Critical Information Consumers

By Mary Alice Anderson

STANDARD 2: The student who is information literate evaluates information critically and competently.

Technology makes finding information relatively easy; but finding the right information is quite a different task. Information seekers no longer have the assurance the available information has been produced, edited, and made accessible by knowledgeable and responsible people. Whether using a book, magazine, online database, or web site, students need to make competent, rational, and valid decisions about the value of the information and its relationship to their needs. Standard 2 defines this information literacy skill using four indicators: the ability to determine accuracy, relevance, and comprehensiveness; the ability to distinguish among fact, point of view, and opinion; the ability to identify inaccurate or misleading information; and the ability to select information appropriate to the problem or question at hand.

Media specialists and teachers accustomed to teaching the research process will recognize these tasks. The importance of these skills has increased as the amount and diversity of available information has increased. All of the lessons in this chapter include one basic critical skill in this age of electronic copying and pasting, that is, the importance of citing sources. Learning to examine the source of information is an important part of the larger process of information evaluation.

Several curriculum areas, including health, social issues, and science, stand out as subject areas where students especially need to examine the information they access. While it may be possible for an adult to determine the validity of a web site, it may be very difficult for students without enough background knowledge to make a good decision. Articles in well-known magazines have the potential to be blatantly inaccurate and biased or otherwise misleading. Library media specialists need to develop and establish instructional practices that move towards a higher level of critical thinking than that involved in simply finding the information.

Joan Haberkorn's lesson titled "Encyclopedia Comparison/Black History Month" offers an excellent introduction to this skill by asking students to compare the information found in two reliable information sources: print and CD-ROM encyclopedias. Information evaluation skills are extended in "Reliable vs. Unreliable Sources" by Kathy and Thom Tobiason, providing additional guided practice in these skills. Working with their teacher and the media specialist, students participate in a group evaluation of specially selected web sites. This information is contrasted with information on a similar topic found in standard print resources. Throughout the process students discuss concepts such as misleading information, and are also guided in the development of their own criteria for assessing information accuracy.

The proficient level of Indicator 3, "explains why inaccurate and misleading information can lead to faulty conclusions" (*Information Power*, p. 15) is highlighted in another lesson authored by Joan Haberkorn. In "Evaluating Internet Resources: Anne Frank Unit" students critically examine Holocaust-related documents that present very different perspectives. This structured activity provides

> **Library media specialists need to develop and establish instructional practices that move towards a higher level of critical thinking than that involved in simply finding the information.**

students with concrete steps that they can follow to evaluate the opinions expressed at different web sites. This lesson could easily be extended into a discussion of how the Internet provides a forum for many other examples of spurious and misleading information. The description of a student proficient in this indicator notes that he or she should "determine how different points of view can influence the facts and opinions presented in controversial issues" (*Information Power*, p. 15). "Mock Senate" by Lesley Farmer gives library media specialists a framework that can be applied to many different content areas. In this lesson, students role play the position a Senator from a specific state would take on a political issue. The activity requires students to reflect on how state issues affect the federal government and to consider how politicians balance the interests of their constituents with the interests of the state or country as a whole.

To help students become critical information consumers, library media specialists need to provide a wide range of resources and introduce students to different kinds of information than those to which they are accustomed. At the basic level of proficiency, Indicator 4 notes that a student should "recognize information that is applicable to a specific information problem or question" (*Information Power*, p. 15). Becky Mather calls on students to consider part of history that is often left out of textbooks in "The Role of American Women in World War II." This challenging and creative lesson is based on a WebQuest created by Mather. In this lesson students search the Internet to locate relevant information resources, and then complete an oral history project. The project culminates with the creation of a web page or PowerPoint presentation. Mather has provided a detailed rubric that teachers, media specialists and students can use in the evaluation process, allowing students to develop their information literacy skills well beyond the basic level.

The description for Standard 2 says that "The student applies these principles insightfully across information sources and formats and uses logic and informed judgment to accept, reject, or replace information to meet a particular need" *(Information Power,* p. 14). As students search, library media specialists and teachers can help students evaluate information through individual conferencing as they work through the research process, promote practices such as note taking instead of copying or cutting/pasting, suggest that students record their progress and thoughts in research logs as they work on projects, and work with teachers to schedule alternating class periods of research and information processing.

Lessons that promote these critical information literacy behaviors are found throughout this edition of Skills for Life. The lessons included in this chapter were selected because they demonstrate instructional strategies that can be applied across many different content areas. Be creative as you adapt these lessons to meet the needs of your students, especially when you consider ways to help students of all ages develop information evaluation skills that go beyond basic levels of proficiency.

Mary Alice Anderson, Media Specialist, Winona (Minnesota) Middle School, Information Power Trainer

TITLE: *Reliable vs. Unreliable Sources*

AUTHOR: Kathy Tobiason, Librarian, and Thom Tobiason, Technology Specialist, The American School in Japan, Tokyo

CURRICULUM AREA: Information Skills

CURRICULUM CONNECTIONS: Preparation for beginning research projects in any subject.

GRADE LEVELS: 4–12

PREREQUISITES: None.

INFORMATION LITERACY STANDARDS FOR STUDENT LEARNING:
Standard 1, Indicator 5
Standard 2, Indicators 1–3

OTHER OUTCOMES/STANDARDS:
Big6: Use of Information—4.2 Extract relevant information
- Student will be able to explain the concept "reliable source."
- Students will develop a rubric for evaluating "reliability" of sources.

MATERIALS/SOURCES NEEDED:
- Computer equipped with Internet access, Web browser and printer—for teacher preparation.

STRATEGIES:
- Provide students with experience in detecting bias, "spin," and disinformation in reporting and presenting information.
- Provide students with experience in identifying balanced coverage.
- Guide students in developing a rubric for assessing reliability of any source—print or electronic.

STEPS:

1 Prior to class, locate web sites sponsored by companies or organizations with a political agenda, for example tobacco company descriptions of the congressional legislation aimed at holding them financially responsible for individual medical expenses. Almost any issue of public policy has Web sites devoted to one side or the other. It is more difficult to find information sources that are balanced than those that are not. For example, you might have students compare the information presented at The Smoker's Club Web site (**http://www.smokersclub.com/**) or the American Smoker's Alliance (**http://www.smokers.org/**) with the Center for Disease Control's TIPS: Tobacco Information and Prevention Source (**http://www.cdc.gov/nccdphp/osh/index.htm**).

2 After asking for permission from the Web site owner or copyright holder, print out examples from these sites and duplicate for students.

3 Locate coverage of the same topic by respected news organizations such as the *New York Times* or *Washington Post*. Check your license agreement to see if you can duplicate the articles for students, or once again ask for permission, then copy the articles for students to use.

4 As a class, combine the information from a dictionary definition of *reliable* and *source* to make a class definition of *reliable source.*

5 Apply the class definition to both sets of information. Look for evidence of bias or "spin" in each example. Discuss the pros and cons of each as a reliable source.

6 In groups of four, discuss the merits of each source and rank them from "most reliable" to "least reliable." (15 minutes).

7 As the groups report their results, create a class chart showing the ratings for each of the sources.

Another good example of bias, or the more current term, spin, that is simple enough for most students is taken from the following journalism textbook: English, Earl, Clarence Hach, and Tom E. Rolnicki. Scholastic Journalism, 8th edition. Ames, Iowa: Iowa State University Press, 1990.

"In the headline 'Congress Budget Snipers Stint Agencies' notice the connotative words *snipers* and *stint*." It's useful to look up the words *sniper* and *stint* and ask students to rephrase the headline in simpler words. Then ask students what they think it means. The results are usually pretty humorous. Ask students to consider how their impression of what happened differs from the headline 'Congress Cut Funds of Agencies.'" (p. 329)

Other examples could be taken from your own local newspapers, and students could be asked to locate additional examples from magazines and newspapers they might have at home. This activity also provides students with an excellent opportunity to use their thesaurus and dictionary skills!

Misinformation is easier for students to understand. An example from their own experience is useful such as, your mother asks, "Did you write Grandma Smith to thank her for your birthday money?" You answer "Yes," even though you haven't finished the note so you can go out and play, promising yourself you will finish the thank-you note later. That's misinformation. It's not a bald-faced lie, but it certainly isn't the whole truth.

WRAP-UP:

■ Based on their experiences in encountering biased information, ask students to brainstorm the questions that they would like to ask a source before receiving information. Some examples might be: Will you profit from the outcome of this event? Will you lose money from the outcome of this event? Do you have a religious belief that influences your perception of this issue?

■ Determine as a group which four questions are the most important. This list of questions forms the basis of a student-generated rubric to use in assessing the reliability of a source.

EVALUATION/CRITIQUE:

Assess the students' effectiveness in evaluating the reliability of sources by giving them the opportunity to repeat the original activity independently using a new topic.

COMMENTS/TIPS/FOLLOW-UP:

Assign students to ask their friends or family members what questions they would ask to determine whether a source is reliable. Discuss instances when respected news organizations might not be reliable sources, such as when they are reporting on themselves.

Some useful sites for helping students learn to evaluate Web-based information include:

Kathy Schrock, Guide for Educators: Critical Evaluation Information
(**http://discoveryschool.com/schrockguide/eval.html**)

Joyce Valenza, Evaluating Web Pages: A WebQuest
(**http://mciunix.mciu.k12.pa.us/~spjvweb/evalwebteach.html**).

Both of these sites provide samples of evaluation rubrics that can be used with students at different grade levels.

Other sites may be useful when working with older students. The focus here is on the standards that journalists have to meet to be reliable. These can be the basis for a rubric to determine reliability in a variety of sources.

Society of Professional Journalists Ethics Page:
http://www.spj.org/ethics/index.htm

Poynter Institute – Online Journalism Ethics Forum:
http://www.poynter.org/research/me/nme/jvnm2.htm

Media and ethics weblinks by Dr. Max Hayes
http://www.ucaqld.com.au/uc/sra/HayesHomePages/MediaEthics.html

TITLE: *Encyclopedia Comparison/Black History Month*

AUTHOR: Joan Haberkorn, Library Media Specialist, Fruita (Colorado) Middle School

CURRICULUM AREA: Information Skills

CURRICULUM CONNECTIONS: Language Arts, Social Studies

GRADE LEVEL: 6–8

PREREQUISITES: Familiarity with print encyclopedias, ability to access information on electronic encyclopedia.

INFORMATION LITERACY STANDARDS FOR STUDENT LEARNING:
Standard 1, Indicators 2, 4, 5
Standard 2, Indicators 1-3
Standard 3, Indicators 2 and 3

BIG 6:
Information Seeking Strategies (2)
Student will know which resources are available

Use of Information (4)
Student will know what can be used from the resources (and which is the better source)

MATERIALS/SOURCES NEEDED:
- Set of print encyclopedias
- Computers and CD-ROM encyclopedias (Note: *World Book* and *Encarta* contain all the names used in this activity)
- Names for students to research and worksheets for comparisons

STRATEGIES:
- Discuss Black History Month with students. Tell them that the activity they will work on today will provide them with an opportunity to learn about an important individual while giving them a tool for assessing sources.
- Point out that they should attempt to find more than one source for any research assignment; one is most likely going to have better information than the other.

STEPS:

■ Distribute and review the student worksheets. Stress that the print encyclopedia should be examined first, so students will be able to use it for comparison with the electronic version.

■ Assign each student (or pair of students, depending on size of class) the name of the person they will research.

■ After students have worked on the assignment, bring them together to discuss the differences they found in the articles in their print and electronic encyclopedias and how they could use this same process for future research (even if they use different sources).

BLACK HISTORY MONTH ACTIVITY

Name: _____

1 Name of person you are researching _____

2 When was he/she born? _____ When did he/she die? _____

3 Why was this person important? _____
_____

4 Compare the information you found in *World Book Encyclopedia* in print, and in *Encarta Encyclopedia* on the computer.

A. Are pictures included? Are they black and white or in color?	
World Book	*Encarta*
B. How long is this article (how many paragraphs)?	
World Book	*Encarta*
C. Find one fact in *World Book* that you did not find in *Encarta*	Find one fact in *Encarta* that you not find in *World Book*.

5 Which of the encyclopedias do you think is better for this assignment? Why?

_____
_____
_____

NAMES FOR STUDENTS TO RESEARCH

Duke Ellington

Marian Anderson

Paul Robeson

Katherine Dunham

James Weldon Johnson

Langston Hughes

Richard Nathaniel Wright

Louis Armstrong

Charlie Parker

Jesse Owens

Bill Russell

James Arthur Baldwin

W.E.B. Du Bois

Mary McLeod Bethune

A. Phillip Randolph

Ralph Johnson Bunche

Charles Richard Drew

Paul Laurence Dunbar

Althea Gibson

TITLE: *Evaluating Internet Resources/Anne Frank Unit*

AUTHOR: Joan Haberkorn, Library Media Specialist, Fruita (Colorado) Middle School

CURRICULUM AREA: Information Skills

CURRICULUM CONNECTIONS: Language Arts, Social Studies

GRADE LEVEL: 8

INFORMATION POWER II STANDARD:
Standard 1, Indicators 4, 5
Standard 2, Indicators 1-4

BIG 6: Use of Information
Student will be able to identify sources by their addresses.
Student will determine point of view in an Internet article.

MATERIALS/SOURCES NEEDED:
■ Overhead projector
■ Copies of Internet articles (used with permission of copyright holder)
■ Worksheets for student evaluation of articles

STRATEGIES:
■ Discuss the selection process for library materials and compare it to the unregulated Internet.
■ Talk about the difference between *fact* and *opinion,* and discuss the relevance of *point of view.*
■ Stress that it is important to find more than one source of information, to learn as much as possible about the authors of the information, and to question the intent and point of view of authors and the documents they use.
■ Addresses for two web examples are included on the Internet Addresses overhead. These sites include documents that students could use to complete this activity but please note that the actual documents should only be duplicated and distributed as hard copies if the copyright holder grants permission. You may need to locate other similar sites in order to find relevant documents that you can obtain permission to use. If you have access to an adequate number of computers, students could read the documents online, avoiding this particular copyright issue.

STEPS:
1 Show students the overhead transparency for Internet Address Endings and explain how these will be the first clues for determining the publisher of the Internet information. Go over endings for the various agencies, with the following caveats:

a. An education site can be used by staff or students to publish their own opinions or viewpoints.

b. A commercial site needs to make a profit; they may sell Internet access, through links, allowing groups and individuals to have sites unregulated by the "host" site, such as AOL.com.

c. An organization must document its nonprofit status.

2 Show the transparency for Internet addresses using the documents the students will be reading. From this transparency point out the following:

a. The **http://** and htm/html at the beginning and end of the address are computer language. They allow sites to be linked.

b. The slashes between segments of the addresses show separate files at the website (think of the Web site as a file cabinet containing many files).

b. The tilde (~) designates an individual using the domain to post his/her Web site. The document may or may not contain information about the individual, but you may be able to find additional information by doing an Internet search.

3 Distribute the Internet articles and inform students they represent opposing viewpoints about the Holocaust. Show them where the address is on the printed copy.

4 Review the evaluation worksheet used to record findings and allow time for students to complete the assignment.

EVALUATION/CRITIQUE:

Follow-up activities should include review as well as application to individual research. Students are evaluated on how well they complete the worksheet.

INTERNET ADDRESS ENDINGS

EDU   education

http://mesa.colorado.edu (Mesa State College)

GOV   government

http://noaa.gov (National Oceanic and Atmospheric Administration)

MIL   military

http://army.mil   (U. S. Army)

COM   commercial

http://mtv.com   (MTV Online)

NET   network

http://csn.net (Colorado Supernet)

ORG   nonprofit organization

http://fruita.org (Fruita Chamber of Commerce)

k12.co.us

ending signifying a public school system, plus the state and country

INTERNET ADDRESSES

EXAMPLE 1:

http://www.holocaust-trc.org/wmp17.htm

http://	Hyper text transfer protocol
www.	World Wide Web
holocaust-trc	Name of domain (organization)
org	Organization
/wmp17.	Folder at the Web site
htm	Hypertext mark-up

EXAMPLE 2:

http://www.wsu.edu/~lpauling/nutshell.html

http://	Hyper text transfer protocol
www.	World Wide Web
wsu.	Washington State University (domain)
edu	Education site
/~lpauling	Individual with own Web page
/nutshell.	Folder in the Web page
html	Hypertext markup language

EVALUATING INTERNET RESOURCES

Name: _____

Examine Examples 1 and 2. Both examples are articles about concentration camps in World War II and were found by searching on the Internet. Answer the questions in the spaces provided.

1 What kind of agency posted the information (education, government, military, commercial, network, or nonprofit organization)?

Example 1	Example 2

2 Was this a publication directly from the agency or was it from an individual? If it was an individual, what was the name?

Example 1	Example 2

3 Give a short summary of the article.

Example 1	Example 2

4 Is the material well written? Is the presentation professional? Tell why or why not.

Example 1	Example 2

5 How could you check for accuracy of the information in the article?

Example 1	Example 2

6 Why do you think the information was posted on the Web? What does the author want you to understand or to believe?

Example 1	Example 2

7 Describe how using the above process could be helpful to you when you are researching the World Wide Web for your Anne Frank project.

_____

_____

_____

_____

_____

_____

TITLE: *Mock Senate*

AUTHOR: Lesley S. J. Farmer, Associate Professor, California State University, Long Beach, California

CURRICULUM AREA: Social studies

CURRICULUM CONNECTION: Any subject area focusing on identifying point of view to inform decision making

GRADE LEVELS: 9–12

PREREQUISITE: Basic debate principles

INFORMATION LITERACY STANDARDS FOR STUDENT LEARNING :
Standard 1, Indicators 2, 4, 5
Standard 2, Indicators 1–4
Standard 3, Indicators 1, 4

BIG6: Task Definition—Identify information needed
■ Students will be able to identify information needed to develop a case debate.

Location and access/Locate sources—Find information and note source
■ Students will be able to locate and select information about state political/economic issues.

Use of Information/Extract relevant information
■ Students will be able to identify perspectives about state political/economic issues.
■ Students will be able to distinguish between fact and opinion.
■ Students will be able to analyze information to make inferences about state's stances on issues.

Synthesis/Organize information from multiple sources—Present the information
■ Students will be able to develop a persuasive argument about a state issue.

MATERIALS/SOURCES NEEDED:
■ Sources about states and state issues
■ Sources about debating techniques

STRATEGIES:
■ The library media specialist or content teacher brainstorms with students about political issues that are state-sensitive.
■ The library media specialist talks with students about government documents and other sources of information about states and state's issues.

■ The library media specialist or content teacher divides students into small collaborative groups. These groups determine individual responsibilities, such as who will gather information about states, information about Senators, information about political issues.

STEPS:

Students form small groups.

■ Students choose a state and a Senator.

■ Students research background information about the state, Senator, and political issues.

■ Students write resolutions about actions to solve state political issues.

■ Students debate political issues, and vote on them.

WRAP-UP:

■ Students discuss states' issues in light of each state and Senator.

■ They determine what overlap between states exists and the federal impact on each issue. How is the federal government affected by state issues? Examples: If Native Americans can now fish the Columbia River in Oregon and Washington, will it affect the Federal Government? (probably not). What if Texas taxed all their oil wells? Will it affect Federal Government? (It probably would in terms of energy sources and foreign policy.)

EVALUATION/CRITIQUE:

■ Students evaluate peer resolutions in terms of accuracy, thoroughness, and persuasiveness of arguments by means of a class-developed rubric or a list of criteria for evaluation.

■ Students vote on resolutions. If students vote for the Senate resolution, it means they find the idea and resolution logical and useful.

COMMENTS/TIPS/FOLLOW-UP:

■ Students compare their resolutions with those of Congress.

■ They discuss the balance between federal and states' rights.

■ They discuss the issues of representation or how well the Senator represented his or her state. How well did the student re-enact the Senator's stance?

BIBLIOGRAPHY OF ELECTRONIC SOURCES:

http://www.thomas.gov   Library of Congress gateway to federal documents

TITLE: *The Role of American Women in World War II*

AUTHOR: Becky Mather, Quality Learning Consultant, Mississippi Bend Area Education Agency, Bettendorf, Iowa

CURRICULUM AREA: U.S. History

CURRICULUM CONNECTIONS: Women's Studies

GRADE LEVELS: 10–12

PREREQUISITES: This is best used as part of a unit on World War II or women's studies.

INFORMATION LITERACY STANDARDS FOR STUDENT LEARNING:
Standard 1, Indicator 5
Standard 2, Indicator 4
Standard 3, Indicator 4

NATIONAL EDUCATIONAL TECHNOLOGY STANDARDS: Standard 2-1, Standard 5-1.

BIG6: 1–6

MATERIALS/SOURCES NEEDED:

■ Internet access

■ Reference materials on World War II and women's issues in general

This activity is derived from a WebQuest I have created. You may view the entire WebQuest with links and other resources at **http://www.muscanet.com/~mather** or **http://www.kn.pacbell.com/wired/fil/pages/webbmather.html**

STRATEGIES:

1 Students are divided by their teacher into groups of four (give or take).

2 Set the stage for the activity using this narrative:
A child is born, given a home and love by her parents, and grows to adulthood. When asked to recount the history of her life, should she merely mention the father's contributions and not the mother's? Can one retell the story of one's life fully, accurately or well, when leaving out the other half of the story?

3 Too often, what passes for history is just a retelling of one side of the past, one half of the story. To really understand who we are today and how we got here, it is necessary to view historical events from multiple perspectives. To do otherwise is to proceed through the rich field of history like a horse with blinders on, seeing only one way, though it is through many paths converging we are led to the present.

4 The purpose of this WebQuest is to allow students to use the of Internet to help loosen these ties that blind us, rather than enlighten us, to "herstory," the history of women in America's past.

THE TASK:

The student's task is to write women back into history, in particular, the history of World War II, and in the process to discover what men and women of today owe to the efforts of the American women who served their country at home, at work, and in the armed forces during World War II.

PROCESS AND RESOURCES:
For the Student:

In this WebQuest you will be working together with a group of students in class to research the role of American women in World War II. Your research will also require you to interview someone from your family or community who can provide a firsthand account of life during the war years. Your choice for your interview should be someone who can provide an additional historical perspective to your work.

You will be expected to use the information you've gathered to create a web page or a PowerPoint presentation detailing the oral history of the person you interviewed, with your research providing background information.

PHASE 1–Background: Something for Everyone

To begin, familiarize yourself with the links under Oral Histories. As a group, follow the lessons provided at the American Memory site on how to conduct oral histories. Keep this information in mind as you explore the topics that follow.

Remember to cite and document the online sources you use to support your research and writings. Refer to the Classroom Connect site for formal citing guidelines

PHASE 2–Looking Deeper from Different Perspectives

1 Your WebQuest team will explore these topics: Women and Work, Women in the Military, Women in Popular Culture.

2 Visit as many web sites as possible and read through the files. If you print out information, underline the passages that you feel are most important. As you look at the files on the computer, take notes on sections you feel are important by typing into a word processor program which allows you to keep your work open and minimized on the screen.

3 Remember to bookmark or copy/paste the URL of the file so you can quickly go back to it if you need to prove your point.

4 Read through the questions carefully. For each set of questions (1, 2, 3, etc.) brainstorm as a team to come up with an hypothesis (see Hypertext dictionary) or conclusion that you feel might best answer the questions.

5 Divide the questions among the team members for research purposes.

6 Each team member should be prepared to report back to the team with his or her findings.

7 As a team, reevaluate your original hypothesis. How accurate were your original answers? What was surprising, what was not?

8 Each team should record its own reflections about what has been learned as part of the self- evaluation.

QUESTIONS:

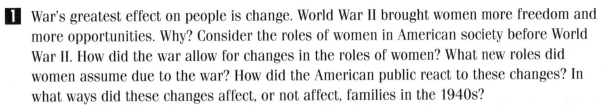

1 War's greatest effect on people is change. World War II brought women more freedom and more opportunities. Why? Consider the roles of women in American society before World War II. How did the war allow for changes in the roles of women? What new roles did women assume due to the war? How did the American public react to these changes? In what ways did these changes affect, or not affect, families in the 1940s?

2 What factors shaped the wartime experiences of American women? Consider ideas such as: Geography (did where women lived make a difference- certain parts of the country, or urban vs. rural); Race or ethnicity (African-American, Native American, German-American, Japanese-American, Jewish, etc.); Economic status (poor, middle class, upper class).

3 Were there certain universal experiences common to all women despite their individual differences?

4 Examine the various ways men and women were portrayed in popular culture of the 1940s (see the links to posters and ads, comics, movies of the 1940s). What conclusions can you draw about the "ideal" man or woman of the 1940s? How were these ideals used to encourage men and women to support the war effort? What conclusions can you draw about the power of advertising to instill patriotism in people? Why was it necessary to "sell" this war effort?

5 It has often been said that wars are not won on the battlefield but rather on the homefront where the efforts and support of the civilian population are vital to a soldier's success. What information can you find that supports this idea? How did American women contribute to American military successes of World War II at home, in the factory and/or in the armed forces?

6 The men returned from the war to find that women had changed. How did the males react to these changes? What adjustments did women have to make when the war ended and the soldiers returned?

7 Compare and contrast the women of the 1940s with the women of today. One commonality would be the prevalence of women in the workplace. Why was this idea of working women not acceptable to most Americans at the end of the war? What fundamental beliefs did Americans hold about women's roles that were not altered by the war? Why do you think this was so? Are these beliefs still common today? If so, why?

These questions will form the foundation of your project which will write women back into the history of World War II.

PHASE 3—Debating, Discussing, and Reaching Consensus

1 Share the information, pictures, facts, and opinions from the Web pages you explored with your teammates. Discuss, from your viewpoint, what you feel is important and should be included as part of your team's fulfillment of the quest to write women back into history.

2 Using what you have learned through your research, as a group, prepare a list of questions to use to interview a relative, acquaintance, neighbor, or community member who lived through the war years of the 1940s.

3 Your group will incorporate these interviews into this project.

PHASE 4–Real World Feedback

This is the last portion of your quest! To demonstrate what you have learned, prepare to publish or post your project or oral history to a project Web site. Alternative assignment: prepare a presentation using PowerPoint software.

Your presentation or project should include your oral history, some kind of visuals (pictures, film, poster, charts, etc.) and your report detailing what you have learned about women in World War II.

Real-world assessment or feedback must come from those whom you seek to interview. Using the information you have discovered about women in World War II, present your research to your interviewees. Can they add to or confirm your research? Do they find contradictions with your work? Use this feedback in assessing your team's effort. How well did you do?

CONCLUSION:

Did what you learned surprise you? How did filling in "the rest of the story" provide you with a better understanding of the history of America and World War II? With what other topics could this quest be used? How do oral histories add to our historical research?

The next time you pick up that history text, remember to ask yourself two fundamental questions: Whose story is being told? And, more importantly, whose story is not?

EVALUATION/ASSESSMENT:

This rubric explains the criteria that will be used to evaluate your project.

CATEGORY	EXEMPLARY	ACCOMPLISHED	DEVELOPED	BEGINNING
RESEARCH	**4.** A variety of WWII print and non-print sources were used and cited correctly.	**3.** More than one type of source (WWII, books, video, etc.) was used, and most sources were correctly cited.	**2.** Several sources were used and cited.	**1.** Only 1 or 2 sources were used and sources were not cited. Plagiarism may be suspected.
TEAMWORK	**4.** The workload was divided and shared equally by all team members.	**3.** All team members did some work.	**2.** Most team members participated in the work.	**1.** One or two people did all or most of the work.
FOCUSED TOPIC	**4.** Clearly defines the topic and goes on to give specific details.	**3.** Describes the topic and gives examples.	**2.** Briefly mentions a topic, but gives few details.	**1.** Information rambles and does not pinpoint a specific topic.
WELL ORGANIZED	**4.** Every section begins with a clearly stated topic sentence, and the sections follow a logical sequence.	**3.** Includes some topic sentences and is somewhat sequential.	**2.** Project has only one topic sentence and its sequence is confusing.	**1.** Lacks topic sentences and has no logical sequence.
CLEAR AND UNDERSTANDABLE	**4.** Easy to read and follow the information.	**3.** Mostly easy to understand.	**2.** Mostly difficult to follow and understand.	**1.** Very difficult to follow.
GRAMMAR AND SPELLING	**4.** All grammar and spelling is correct.	**3.** Only one or two errors in spelling and grammar.	**2.** A few grammar and/or spelling errors.	**1.** Very frequent grammar and/or spelling errors.
MULTI-MEDIA	**4.** Excellent use of visuals, text and sound. Shows creative multimedia skills.	**3.** Good use of visuals, text, and sound. Shows good multimedia skills.	**2.** Some visuals, text, and sound. Shows some multimedia skills.	**1.** Lacks visuals, text, and sound. Shows little or no multimedia skills.

CHAPTER 3

Presenting Information Creatively

By Mary Alice Anderson

STANDARD 3: The student who is information literate uses information accurately and creatively.

Using information is at the heart of the information literacy process. Students access information in order to use it. Using information means learning from it by reading, viewing, or listening. Working with it requires organizing information, making it part of one's own knowledge, and presenting the results of the learning experience to others. This final step means communicating or presenting that information in an appropriate format, which also involves solving problems and making decisions.

In the past, communicating information usually meant a "report." Today changes in education and a shift toward project-based, constructivist, and active learning require more than the traditional paper-and-pencil report. Posters, models, role playing, speeches, video productions, word processed documents, and time lines all provide opportunities for students to be actively involved in the learning process. Newer information presentation methods, such as multimedia or Web-based communications, offer even more interactive opportunities for students. The media center is no longer an information-gathering place but also an information-producing place. Activities in this chapter have students create travel brochures, business cards, links pages, and PowerPoint presentations. The authors of these lessons demonstrate exciting ways to incorporate new and old technologies into the information literacy process.

Media specialists may now find new partners in teachers who have shied away from the research process. Media specialists can collaborate with teachers to develop instructional activities that stress the entire information process rather than just the technical skills involved in creating the final product. For teachers accustomed to the research process, it may mean thinking about the process in a different way. The traditional research paper still fits, but so does the HyperStudio project. Teachers and media specialists who are accustomed to concrete, sequential research processes will learn to work with a process that is less structured. Both require critical thinking, synthesis, and organization. For students, the information literacy process means higher levels of motivation, more opportunities to enjoy the process, and more success using criteria that they have been involved in creating.

Indicator 1 for Standard 3 states that the student "organizes information for practical application" (Information Power, p. 19). Students at the basic level will be able to describe alternative methods of organizing information, while students at the proficient or exemplary levels will actually be able to organize information in new and effective ways. Several of the lessons in this chapter provide models for organizing information for effective use. "Using Simple Correlations in Databases" by Thom Tobiason promotes practical information organization. Here, students take information from a variety of sources and organize it into a computerized database in order to perform a variety of hypothesis-testing activities. While Tobiason uses data on the countries of the world, creative media specialists and teachers could easily adapt this lesson to other content areas. In "Money Makes the World Go Round," Lisa Muir suggests that students research the cost of various items in other countries of the world. While

> For teachers accustomed to the research process, it may mean thinking about the process in a different way. The traditional research paper still fits, but so does the HyperStudio project.

Muir utilizes a paper-and-pencil method of organizing this information to plan a vacation, this activity could easily be extended to utilize a spreadsheet. Identifying and verifying information to ensure accuracy are additional key features of these lessons. The suggested activities for both provide an environment that will help students achieve Indicator 2, "Integrates new information into one's own knowledge" (Information Power, p. 19).

Newer methods of presenting information provide opportunities for teacher and media specialist collaboration. The media center can be used to showcase projects in a variety of formats, and media specialists can suggest alternative methods of information gathering and presentation to teachers and students.

Indicator 3, "Applies information in critical thinking and problem solving," and Indicator 4, "Produces and communicates information and ideas in appropriate formats," open the door for media specialists to work with students to synthesize information and communicate the results of their work in new and exciting ways. Exemplary projects, which require students to creatively use information for problem solving and select appropriate formats for communicating results, are within the reach of all students. Students who experience "Our Heritage: Lessons From Past Generations" by Kathryn Brown will get a chance to synthesize information from oral history sources, reference materials, and fiction. The final product of this activity will be a print or multimedia anthology of stories placed in the media center. After participating in "Multimedia Career Exploration" by Patricia Kolencik, students will have learned how to create a graphic organizer of their chosen career field and even produce their own personalized business card. Both lessons offer several suggested methods of evaluating these creative products.

Assessing the effectiveness of the information skills process (from information access through presentation) is an important component of this standard. Assessment rubrics can involve the entire information process, not just the final product, and they can involve learners, teachers, and media specialists. In fact, self-assessment is highlighted throughout this chapter. "Multimedia Career Exploration" integrates assessment from the initial stages of the activity by including a learning log with space for teacher/library media specialist feedback, a career reflection and self-evaluation instrument, a peer assessment rubric, and a teacher/library media specialist weekly assess-

ment rubric. Lesley Farmer also suggests peer evaluation in "Hypermedia Sports Physics." All of the rubrics and assessment models included with the lessons in this chapter could be adapted to different content areas and products. Developing evaluation and assessment rubrics is a new responsibility for many media specialists. Practice using pre-created rubrics will help to build confidence in working with students as they develop their own rubrics.

Media specialists will see that Standard 3 provides exciting opportunities; the lessons presented here illustrate just some of them.

Mary Alice Anderson, Media Specialist, Winona (Minnesota) Middle School, Information Power Trainer.

TITLE: *Simple Correlations in Databases*

AUTHOR: Thomas Tobiason, Elementary Technology Specialist, The American School in Japan, Tokyo

CURRICULUM AREA: Information Skills

CURRICULUM CONNECTION: Social Studies

GRADE LEVELS: 4–8

INFORMATION LITERACY STANDARDS FOR STUDENT LEARNING:
Standard 3, Indicators 1, 3

OTHER OUTCOMES/STANDARDS:
Big6: Synthesis—Making sense of information

LEARNING EXPECTATIONS/OUTCOMES:
- Student will be able to sort a database on any given field.
- Student will be able to construct simple correlation hypotheses.
- Student will be able to test a correlation hypothesis by sorting a database.
- Student will be able to evaluate the results of the hypothesis testing and decide whether the hypothesis is "true" or not.

MATERIALS/SOURCES NEEDED:
- One computer per student or pair of students
- Internet access or almanacs
- Spreadsheet program, database program, or word processor that will sort records

STRATEGIES:
- Students collect data themselves and help assemble the database.
- Teacher or media specialist demonstrates simple database correlations to the whole class.
- Students investigate a teacher-chosen hypothesis and check the results.
- Students then undertake their own investigations.

STEPS:
The description below assumes an investigation into countries of the world. This lesson could also concern states of the United States, provinces of Canada, and so on. Sources of data would need to be identified.

1 Assign countries to students or groups of students. Also assign what data is to be collected. If Internet access is available, go to the CIA World Fact Book.
(http://www.odci.gov/cia/publications/factbook/index.html)

2 Students locate and record data on their assigned country and assemble the data into a database. Take student-found data and enter it into the database. Save the database and make copies of it (it is also a good idea to make the database file read-only).

3 Teacher or media specialist models hypothesis testing using demonstration and discussion.

4 The teacher and/or media specialist introduces the meaning of two fields in the database, say, *infant mortality* (infants who die who are less than one year old per 1000 population) and *GDP* (gross domestic product). The teacher then wonders out loud if countries with the highest GDPs will also have the lowest infant mortalities. If this is so, this is called a correlation; that is, high GDP tends to go with low infant mortality. The teacher then formalizes this with a hypothesis: high GDP goes with low infant mortality.

5 To test the hypothesis, students sort their databases on GDP first using the high to low option (Z-A). Write down the names of the countries with the nine highest GDPs. Next, sort the database on infant mortality from lowest to highest (A-Z). Write down the names of the countries with the nine lowest infant mortality rates.

6 Mark which countries "fit the hypothesis," that is, are on both lists. Countries on both lists "fit the hypothesis," because they have both high GDP and low infant mortality compared with other countries. The results can be reported as "x out of 9" support the hypothesis, and "y out of 9" do not support the hypothesis. We could say the correlation is strong if 9 out of 9 support the hypothesis, and weak if 5 out of 9 support the hypothesis.

7 The final step is to try to explain the results. Is the result what you expected? Does this result suggest another investigation? Say, does GDP go with death rate? Or life expectancy?

8 Teacher-assigned hypothesis (guided practice): Assign two fields of the database to check for a correlation. Ask the students which fields should be sorted in which order to find out if the hypothesis is true. The students attempt to do the sorting and recording on their own. The results are compared for the whole class to check against.

9 Student investigation (independent practice): Students make up their own hypotheses. Students complete the investigation into possible correlations. Students report the results and optionally write up their findings in paragraph form.

WRAP-UP:

The teacher or media specialist points out that this method of correlation analysis is used broadly by many organizations. Health records are sorted by zip code to reveal areas with abnormal disease distributions. The United Nations has people devoted to investigating these correlations. How does your country stack up against the world in these categories?

EVALUATION/CRITIQUE:

If students can create a hypothesis, sort the database, record the results, and decide if the hypothesis is true or false, they have been successful. If students are left troubled or concerned that some of the hypotheses don't make sense, good! The world is like that. But, their prior work should still show that they did create a hypothesis, sort a database, record results, and come to a conclusion even if wrong or inconclusive.

COMMENTS/TIPS/FOLLOW-UP:

■ Create a sheet to help students formulate hypotheses and record results. The following is a model:

The Question: Are _____ and _____ related?

The Hypothesis: Does (low high) _____ go with (low high) _____ ?

List of (low high) _____   List of (low high) _____

■ The whole world database will give you different results than a specified region will give you. For the Middle East, for instance, the first example cited above (GDP and infant mortality) has no correlation at all. The countries of the Middle East with the largest GDPs also have the highest infant mortalities. Why? This may be an interesting way to look at the differences between regions of the world or levels of industrialization.

TITLE: *Money Makes the World Go Around*

AUTHOR: Lisa Muir, Islamic Saudi Academy, Fairfax, Virginia

CURRICULUM AREA: Civics

CURRICULUM CONNECTIONS: Geography, Math, Economics

GRADES: 7–8

PREREQUISITES: Students should have experience using a calculator for basic math functions.

INFORMATION LITERACY STANDARDS FOR STUDENT LEARNING:
Standard 1, Indicators 1, 5
Standard 3, Indicators 1, 2

OTHER OUTCOMES/STANDARDS:
BIG6: Location and Access/Find information within sources
Use of information/Examine information in sources
Synthesis/Organize information from multiple sources

MATERIALS/SOURCES NEEDED:
- Newspapers: Washington Post (US), Daily Mail, Daily Telegraph (UK)
- AJR Newslink at **http://ajr.newslink.org/** has numerous links to newspapers, magazines and other news sources from many countries.
- Almanacs or Encyclopedia
- Calculators
- Worksheet
- Maps or atlas
- Two class sessions

STRATEGIES:
- Tell students the challenge is to find out how much money you actually have if you are visiting the United Kingdom (after exchanging your U.S. dollars) and how far will that money go if you need to purchase items for daily use.

STEPS:
- Distribute the questionnaire to the class and have them complete Part 1.
- Show examples of money from around the United Kingdom (or other country of your choice).
- Explain process of exchange rate and conversion for money between the United States and the United Kingdom.

■ Show students how to convert money using the math functions of multiplication or division .

> **EXAMPLE 1:** Ten dollars divided by the exchange rate (1.5) will give the amount in pounds.
> $10 / 1.5 = £ 6.66

> **EXAMPLE 2:** Ten pounds multiplied by the exchange rate (1.5) will give the dollars.
> £ 10 x 1.5 = $15

■ Ask students, "Where are you able to find out the present exchange rate for pounds and dollars?" Answers you are looking for include:

Daily Newspapers
The Internet
Travel Agents
Airports (International)

■ Make photocopies of rate charts available or, if computers are available, log on to the Web site (**www.xe.net/currency**)

■ Have students identify the exchange rate for the United Kingdom.

■ Using skills learned in the exchange rate and conversion section, students are asked to calculate the cost of five items based on the price in America. This will become a work sheet presented in table format (see work sheet Part 2).

■ Upon completion of the first task, students should find the actual cost of the items. (Note: this information can be found in advertisements/articles from various United Kingdom newspapers: Daily Mail, Daily Express, Daily Telegraph).

DISCUSSION OF FINDINGS:

■ Are the predicted prices the same as the actual prices?

■ What could cause there to be a difference between the two prices?

■ Could you say that your results would be true for all items in the UK?

■ Could you also apply these findings as a rule for other countries?

■ Could you use your findings for planning a vacation this summer?

EVALUATION:

■ The library media specialist redistributes the class's original questionnaire and asks them to answer the questions again based on what they have learned.

■ The library media specialist will conduct a discussion and guide students toward making comparisons based on what they originally thought they knew and what they now know after the research process.

■ Participation in the discussions, conversion forms and questionnaires will be evaluated by the library media specialist for content and understanding of how to convert money sums.

WRAP-UP:

■ Each student will plan a two-week holiday of his or her choice to a foreign country. Students will have a budget of $1,000 and no credit cards. Students will have to answer the following questions:

> How much will it cost to get there?
> Where can I stay?
> What is the exchange rate?
> How long will my money last?
> What can a tourist do?
> Will I have a good time with this amount of money with this country?

■ Students will make a travel brochure designed to appeal to prospective travelers.

■ The travel brochures will be evaluated by the library media specialist and class based on the following: lists of exchange rates, places to visit and cost of hotels, flights, and key items. Assessment of student learning is interwoven with teaching and occurs through teacher observations of students at work and through student exhibitions and portfolios, promoting constructivist principles of teaching and learning.

TIPS/FOLLOW-UP:

■ The library media specialist can use British newspapers with the class to discuss similarities and differences in presenting information, displaying advertisements (how the ads differ from ours or how the ads catch our eye—or don't) or compare the layouts of those newspapers to ours.

■ The library media specialist can also use the newspapers to compare terminology (for example: Is saying "to rent" the same as "to let"?) and spellings (*tyre* or *tire*, *aeroplane* or *airplane*?)

STUDENT WORKSHEET

PART 1: Try to answer these questions based on what you already know.

- What is the currency used in the United Kingdom?
- How many coins are there in the United States currency?
- How many coins are there in the United Kingdom currency?
- Have you ever been to the United Kingdom?
- What is worth more $5.00 or £ 5-00?
- Where can you find the value of money from another country?
- Where can you obtain foreign money?
- What are the taxes for your state?
- What are the taxes for the United Kingdom?

PART 2:

ITEM	U.S. PRICE	PRICE BASED ON EXCHANGE RATE	ACTUAL PRICE
CD			
Hair dryer			
1 dozen eggs			

TITLE: *Our Heritage: Lessons from Past Generations*

AUTHOR: Kathryn K. Brown, Graduate Student, James Madison University, Harrisonburg, Virginia

CURRICULUM AREA: English

CURRICULUM CONNECTIONS: Information skills, Social Studies, U.S. History

GRADE LEVELS: 7–9

PREREQUISITES:
■ Interview skills, including formulation of questions, selecting a person to interview, and compiling the results
■ Tape recording skills
■ Creative writing skills
■ Research skills, including database, literature, and Internet searches

INFORMATION LITERACY STANDARDS FOR STUDENT LEARNING:
Standard 3, Indicators 1–4

LEARNING EXPECTATIONS/OUTCOMES:

1 RESEARCH: Students will learn about U.S. history from the 1940s to the present by exploring the major personalities, results, and impacts of events such as World War II, the Cold War, the Civil Rights movement, the Korean and Vietnam Wars, and Watergate by developing an understanding of the experiences of people who were there. By researching the time period in which their selected event occurred, they will develop skills for historical analysis.

2 PRODUCT: Students will read a variety of fiction and nonfiction as part of their research. They must organize the information they have collected into an interesting written and oral presentation, which will be shared with classmates. They will utilize interviewing techniques to gain information.

MATERIALS/SOURCES NEEDED:
■ Internet access
■ Writing paper and utensils
■ Tape recorder

STRATEGIES:
■ ASK QUESTIONS: Who am I? How did the lives of my family members affect me? How has the world changed, and how might it change in the future? How can an understanding of the lives of my grandparents affect the beliefs and values that I consider important?

■ By answering these questions, students will make a connection between the lives of those who preceded them and their own lives and the problems they face. This connection will help the student to develop his or her own belief and value systems and will help to develop the student's own identity.

STEPS:

1 During class, students will brainstorm about events from the 1940s to the present. The teacher and media specialist will develop a time line, using the references that are necessary to accurately record dates. This activity will give students information about events their grandparents may have experienced and will give them insight into the interview questions they will ask.

2 Students may work singly or in groups to develop interview questions surrounding a particular event or time period.

3 Students will then interview parents, grandparents, great-grandparents, aunts, uncles, friends, or neighbors to learn about members of previous generations and the lives they led.

4 The student will select a family member from their grandparents' or great-grandparents' generation who had an experience between 1940 and the present that is of interest to the student. For example, a great-grandparent may have been at Pearl Harbor, or may have been at home when the attack on Pearl Harbor occurred. A grandparent may have participated in protests against the Vietnam War. A relative may have been in the audience for Martin Luther King's "I Have a Dream" speech. Adopted children may use a member of their biological or adoptive families, and students who cannot or do not wish to research their own families may use a "substitute" family.

5 The student will demonstrate research strategies by using databases, nonfiction and reference books to locate information about the period of time and event. For example, if the student has selected the topic of a person's life during President Kennedy's assassination, he or she might use databases to locate and review newspaper articles about the assassination and the reactions to it. Reference books will give background information regarding John F. Kennedy, the assassination, the investigation, Lee Harvey Oswald, and Lyndon B. Johnson. Biographies of President Johnson might be used if the focus is the political transition after the assassination.

6 Students will obtain background information for the period or event by reading historical fiction. The media specialist will develop suggested reading lists, bulletin boards, and provide book talks to assist the students with book location and to excite the students regarding their projects. Guest speakers, such as authors of historical fiction, persons who have interesting stories to tell, or whom the students have selected to interview might be invited to share their experiences with the class.

7 The interviews, information, and historical fiction will be compiled into a short story with the selected individual as the central character. The story itself does not need to be true but should be historically accurate.

8 The story will be read or acted out for the student's classmates.

9 The stories will be compiled into an anthology, which will be displayed in the media center for the enjoyment of other students, parents, and faculty.

EVALUATION/CRITIQUE:

- The student will be evaluated on historical accuracy, composition, quality of writing, use of resources, and the presentation of the project.
- Points are awarded if the historical content is accurate, and deducted if there are inaccuracies. Students obtain points for the number of references used (including the fiction books) and for the quality of information obtained from the interviews.
- The composition should be the thoughts and imagination of the student, with original work receiving the highest marks. Points are deducted if the idea is not original or if the work is copied from a reference or from someone else. Writing should reflect correct spelling and grammar, and should hold the interest of the reader.
- Information obtained from the research should be synthesized into an original story. The presentation should be interesting and entertaining and should educate the audience about the event.
- Sources must be cited correctly, using a standard format such as MLA.
- The teacher and media specialist will then compare their point tallies and decide on a grade.

COMMENTS/TIPS/FOLLOW-UP:

The National Council of Social Studies (NCSS) has written that historical perspective is important in the development of one's own identity by understanding his or her place in time and location. Students must develop a historical perspective in order to analyze the issues and problems that confront them today and will confront them in the future. According to the NCSS:

> The study of history allows learners to understand their place in time and location. The knowledge base of historical content drawn from United States and world history provides the basis from which learners develop historical understanding and competence in ways of historical thinking. Historical thinking skills enable learners to evaluate evidence, develop comparative and causal analyses, interpret the historical record, and construct sound historical arguments and perspectives on which informed decisions in contemporary life can be based. Historical understandings define what learners should know about the history of their nation and of the world. These understandings are drawn from the record of human aspirations, strivings, accomplishments, and failures in at least five spheres of human activity: the social, political, scientific/technological, economic, and cultural (philosophical/religious/aesthetic). They also provide learners the historical perspectives necessary to analyze contemporary issues and problems confronting citizens today. (National Council for Social Studies, **http://peabody.vanderbilt.edu/depts/tandl/faculty/Myers/standards.html**; online, available 2/25/99).

TITLE: *Creating a Links Page*

AUTHOR: Kathy Tobiason, Librarian and Thom Tobiason, Technology Specialist, The American School in Japan, Tokyo

CURRICULUM AREA: Information Skills

CURRICULUM CONNECTIONS: Links pages can be used in a variety of ways in almost any subject. They make excellent electronic bibliographies, resource organizers, and unit home pages.

GRADE LEVELS: 7–12

PREREQUISITES: Experience using a search engine to access resources on the World Wide Web.

INFORMATION LITERACY STANDARDS FOR STUDENT LEARNING:
Standard 3, Indicators 1, 4
Standard 4, Indicator 2

OTHER OUTCOMES/STANDARDS:
BIG6:
Synthesis /Students will be able to create a page of active Internet links to serve as a resource organizer or electronic bibliography on a relevant topic.

MATERIALS/SOURCES NEEDED:
- Computers with Internet access and browser
- HTML editor software such as Front Page, Page Mill, or Netscape Composer
- Projection device or large screen display

STEPS:

1 The library media specialist displays an example of a links page and demonstrates how it works.

2 Ask students to brainstorm some ways that such a page could be useful to them. Possible answers: collecting sites on favorite topics, organizing Web resources for a report, bibliographies.

3 Students brainstorm topics for their links pages and select a topic with approval of library media specialist or classroom teacher. Topics could also be selected based on an assignment by the classroom teacher.

4 On the display computer, the library media specialist models the steps for creating a blank HTML page to receive links. Students follow each step right after it is shown:

    a. Open an HTML editor such as Front Page.

    b. At the File menu, choose New.

    c. Choose "normal page" as the template.

    d. Type the topic of the page as a headline.

e. Name the page by choosing "Save As" from the File menu.

f. Give the page the same name as the topic.

g. Minimize the page.

5 On the display computer, the library media specialist models the steps for "capturing" the URL from a Web page. Students follow each step right after it is shown:

a. Open the browser and access a search engine such as Alta Vista.

b. Use the topic or related keywords to locate useful Web sites.

c. Highlight the URL of the chosen Web page. Choose "copy" from the Edit menu to "capture" the URL.

d. Minimize the browser.

6 On the display computer, the library media specialist models the steps for saving the URL to the links page. Students follow each step right after it's shown:

a. Maximize the links page.

b. Type the title of the webpage being captured.

c. Beneath the title, paste the URL by using "paste" from the Edit menu.

d. Save the links page and minimize.

7 Once the process has been demonstrated, the library media specialist assists students while they continue to move between the links page and the browser capturing and pasting URLs for links.

WRAP-UP:

■ Ask a student to volunteer his or her links page to be used as an example. On the display computer, use the Open file of the browser to access the student's links page from a disk or a shared server.

■ Ask students which Web site looks the most interesting based on the title. Click on the links that go with that title.

■ Demonstrate that by clicking on various links the Web sites can be accessed. Explain that by capturing "live" links and pasting them onto an HTML page, the links are active without any further effort.

■ By using the steps they have followed in this lesson, students are now able to create a Web page of their own with active links to Web sites they have chosen and deemed as valuable.

EVALUATION/CRITIQUE:

Assess the students' ability to create links pages by assigning them a new topic and asking them to work independently during a second class session.

COMMENTS/TIPS/FOLLOW-UP:

■ Once the technical skill of creating a links page has been mastered, the opportunity exists to move into higher-order thinking. For instance, discussing standards for evaluation and selection of Web sites: What makes a Web site worthy of inclusion on a links page?

■ Developing a rubric for site evaluation is another worthwhile class activity. Discussing the topic of reliable sources would be especially relevant in the context of selecting Web sites for a links page.

INSTRUCTIONAL GUIDE 16

TITLE: *Multimedia Career Exploration*

AUTHOR: Patricia Kolencik, Teacher-Librarian, North Clarion High School, Tionesta, Pennsylvania

CURRICULUM AREA: Career Education

CURRICULUM CONNECTIONS: Career investigation in any curricular area

GRADE LEVELS: 7–12

PREREQUISITES: Basic knowledge of
■ word processing skills
■ Internet search skills
■ desktop publishing skills

INFORMATION LITERACY STANDARDS FOR STUDENT LEARNING:
Standard 1, Indicators 1–4
Standard 2, Indicator 4
Standard 3, Indicators 1–4

LEARNING EXPECTATIONS/OUTCOMES:
Students will demonstrate their ability to access a variety of technological and information resources to collect, organize, analyze, and present career information in a meaningful multimedia presentation.

MATERIALS/SOURCES NEEDED:
■ Internet access
■ Career books
■ Encyclopedias
■ Career software
■ Bibliography of print and electronic resources for career investigation (prepared by librarian)
■ Paper, business cards for printer (optional)

STRATEGIES:
1. Students explore career counseling resources.
2. Students make career decision and seek library media specialist and teacher approval.
3. Students design a graphic organizer of related career fields.

4 Students research the nature of the work, educational requirements, salary, working conditions, and job outlook by completing career exploration data sheet. (See worksheet 1. This data sheet is a crucial part of the assignment as the data collected is used to develop the narrative for the multimedia presentation and business card design.)

5 Students plan and design a multimedia presentation (see worksheets 2 and 3) and examples of business cards.

6 Students present their work to the class and distribute a sample business card.

At the end of every class period, students will complete a daily log sheet.

EXTENSION ACTIVITIES:

- Write a classified job advertisement.
- Conduct an interview with a person in that career field.
- Job "shadow"
- Make an on-the-job video.
- Resume-writing activities
- Conduct or attend a career fair.
- Create a job portfolio.
- Creative writing assignment

EVALUATION:

- Rubric scored by teacher and library media specialist
- Peer assessment
- Reflection assessment by student

CAREER EXPLORATION DATA SHEET

DIRECTIONS: Using the Career Resources Bibliography, complete each section by taking notes. Be specific when recording your facts. This data will be used as a guide for developing the narrative for your computer slide show. You can elaborate when writing the text for your slides on the planning sheets provided. You must use a variety of print and electronic resources. Under each section, label your source of information. This information will be used to prepare the credit bibliography at the end of your slide show.

Describe your field of interest, i.e., Medicine, Armed Services, Banking, Computers, etc. Source:	Specify the exact career or occupation you would like to investigate in the field. e.g., teacher: secondary. Source:	Briefly describe other related occupations which could be performed with the same training. Source:
Describe the responsibilities of an employee in this occupation (what specific tasks would you perform?). Source:	Describe the usual working conditions for this position. Source:	List the courses you need to take or the special training or education requirements you would need to have for this occupation. [Hint: include length of training, degree, etc.] Source:
What would your beginning salary be? What additional benefits (e.g. bonus pay, med. insurance, travel, vacation) might be offered as incentives? Source:	Describe the possibilities for advancement. (If applicable) Source:	Current employment outlook: Source:

CAREER EXPLORATION DATA SHEET

List 5 schools offering training for your occupation.	List 5 potential employers within our area.	Do you know anyone who does this kind of work? Did that person influence your decision?
Source:	Source:	Source:
If applicable, draw the special logo associated with your profession. If no formal logo is associated with your profession, create an appropriate one for use in your slide show and on your business card.	List some advantages of this occupation.	List some disadvantages of this occupation.
Source:	Source:	Source:
Would you wear a special uniform? If so, describe it.	Why did you choose this occupation?	List 3 reasons why you would recommend this career to others.
Source:		

SLIDE SHOW STORYBOARD PLANNER

Name_____   Date_____

Career:_____

DIRECTIONS: Lay out the story of your slide show here. Make notes and sketches that summarize what each slide will contain.

SLIDE 1	SLIDE 2	SLIDE 3
NOTES	NOTES	NOTES
SLIDE 4	SLIDE 5	SLIDE 6
NOTES	NOTES	NOTES

SLIDE SHOW SLIDE DETAILED WORKSHEET

Name_____   Date_____

Career:_____

Directions: Sketch what you want the slide to look like in the box. Be sure to include titles and where any text will be located. Write the text in the space provided below.

LOG SHEET

Name_____   Date_____

I need someone to help me_____
_____

I am confused about_____
_____

I do not understand_____
_____

I am/am not satisfied with my progress so far because_____
_____

Tomorrow I plan to_____
_____

TEACHER/LIBRARY MEDIA SPECIALIST FEEDBACK:

A resource we think might help you is_____
_____

You might try_____ because_____
_____

You might change_____ because_____
_____

We will meet with you to discuss_____ on_____

TEACHER/LIBRARY MEDIA SPECIALIST WEEKLY ASSESSMENT RUBRIC

TASK	EXCELLENT	SATISFACTORY	NEEDS IMPROVEMENT
1 Effectively uses a variety of resources to gather information (both print and electronic).			
2 Rationale for career selection is sound.			
3 Records information accurately.			
4 Summarizes and demonstrates an understanding of both the preparation required and the work activities associated with the career.			
5 Accurately depicts career field in graphic organizer.			
6 Reflects upon presentation.			
7 Meets deadlines.			

PEER ASSESSMENT RUBRIC:

Classmates will evaluate each other's career presentation using the following feedback form.

Name of speaker_____

Career_____

What do you think the speaker has learned about this career?

_____

_____

_____

_____

_____

_____

Do you think the speaker is developing an appropriate understanding of this career? Why or why not?

_____

_____

_____

_____

_____

_____

_____

CAREER REFLECTION AND SELF EVALUATION

Which source of information did you find to be the most valuable in helping you make your decision? (Write your answer in correct bibliographic format following MLA standards.)

_____

_____

_____

What did you learn from that source that helped you select your career?

_____

_____

_____

What do you know about your skills and abilities that makes this a good career choice for you to pursue?

_____

_____

_____

If you pursue this career, what effect (benefits and challenges) might it have on your

Personal life?_____

Family life?_____

Community life?_____

What are the most important things you've learned about this career?

_____

_____

_____

What have you learned about the preparation required for this career?

_____

_____

_____

What have you learned about the type of work (on the job activities) associated with this career?

_____

_____

_____

Are there any additional questions you need to investigate?

_____

_____

_____

Self-Evaluation: What aspect of your presentation did you feel was most effective? Why?

_____

_____

_____

What aspect(s) of your presentation would you like to improve?

_____

_____

_____

TITLE: *Hypermedia Sports Physics*

AUTHOR: Lesley S. J. Farmer, Associate Professor, California State University, Long Beach

CURRICULUM AREA: Physics

CURRICULUM CONNECTION: Health, Physical Education, Science

PREREQUISITE: Basic knowledge of physics and sports; experience with hypermedia authoring tools (desirable)

GRADE LEVELS: 9–12

INFORMATION LITERACY STANDARDS FOR STUDENT LEARNING:
Standard 2, Indicator 4
Standard 3, Indicators 1, 4
Standard 5, Indicators 2, 3

OTHER OUTCOMES/STANDARDS:
BIG6: Location and Access/Locate sources/Find information within the source
■ Students will be able to locate information about physics principles and sports.

Use of Information/Extract relevant information
■ Students will be able to determine which physical principles are associated with sports actions.

Synthesis/Organize information from multiple sources/Present the information
■ Students will be able to sequence information logically.
■ Students will be able to link visual and written information.
■ Students will be able to create a hypermedia presentation about physics principles in sports.

MATERIALS/SOURCES NEEDED:
■ Resources on sports and physics
■ Authoring tools such as PowerPoint or HyperStudio

STRATEGIES:
■ Library media specialist or content teacher discusses physics principles related to a sports action with students. The easiest method is to take one action, such as hitting a baseball and analyze various physics principles, such as the "sweet spot" of a bat, the velocity of the thrown ball, and the angle of impact.
■ Library media specialist or content teacher divides class into small collaborative groups (2–3 persons). Have students divide responsibilities (for example, one to do layout for the authoring

program, another to do research, and another to apply the physics principles to sports).

STEPS:

- Students choose a sport and a specific action.
- Students research the physics principles that relate to the sports action.
- Students sequence the physics principles relating to the sports action.
- Students develop a step-by-step hypermedia presentation illustrating the physics principles relating to the sports action.

WRAP-UP:

Students compare physics principles across actions and draw conclusions about them.

EVALUATION/CRITIQUE:

Students evaluate peers' hypermedia presentations in terms of accuracy, soundness of physics principles, thoroughness, and clarity.

COMMENTS/TIPS/FOLLOW-UP:

This project can be done on several levels. Only one student in the group needs to be a strong hypermedia "author." Others can scan in diagrams and write textual information. Sophisticated hypermedia creators may want to animate the actions.

BIBLIOGRAPHY OF ELECTRONIC SOURCES:

Human Kinetics
http://www.humankinetics.com/

Slam Dunk Science
http://www.scire.com/sds/sdsmenu.html

Sport! Science @the Exploratorium
http://www.exploratorium.edu/sports/

Some of the Olympics-related sites also discuss the physics principles of sports.
A good reference book is *Encyclopedia of Sports Science*.

Independent Learning

CHAPTER 4

Promoting Lifelong Learning

By Alice Yucht

STANDARD 4: The student who is an independent learner is information literate and pursues information related to personal interests.

W e've all seen it happen: from the kid who "never knew the library had stuff about pets" to the self-motivated weather expert who recommends new resources he's discovered on his own. According to *Information Power: Building Partnerships for Learning,* the student who meets this standard "actively and independently seeks information to enrich understanding of career, community, health, leisure, and other personal situations." This information seeking can cover the full range of individual interests, from looking at magazine pictures about a new TV star to searching for the latest data on medical treatments for AIDS. The student who is an independent learner also "constructs meaning-

ful personal knowledge based on that information and communicates that knowledge accurately and creatively across the range of information formats." In other words, students don't just gather information, they also evaluate what they've found in order to share what they've learned with others.

Personal interest has always been one of the best motivators for active learning. The student who truly cares about his topic will always put more effort into its pursuit. When students can restructure the data they've acquired into a new product through which to share this knowledge, they are able to both internalize their understanding of the information-seeking activity and to demonstrate their ability to convey what they've learned. Teachers and library media specialists need to capitalize on this aspect of self-motivation to encourage students to develop the skills they will need for the rest of their lives.

There are two indicators for Standard 4, each with three levels of proficiency—basic, proficient, and exemplary. Indicator 1 states that the student "seeks information related to various dimensions of personal well-being" (*Information Power*, p. 23). On the most basic level, the student "occasionally seeks information" but makes no major effort to find it. This can include glancing at current magazines, browsing through a new book on an interesting topic, or a brief information search for some basic data. The proficient student "generally goes beyond one's own knowledge" by looking at a few more possibilities, while the exemplary student "explores a range of sources," seeking as much information as possible.

Librarians are always providing opportunities for students to attain the basic level of Indicator 1 through displays and demonstrations of new materials available. Many of the individual research questions we deal with cover the proficient level, as students seek additional information to buttress what they already know on a topic. Exemplary-level students extend their searches for as much information as they can find on a topic, comparing and contrasting what they already know with what they now find. Mary Alice Anderson's "Famous People from your State or City" requires an exemplary level of information-seeking, as students explore local history files and a variety of print and online materials to gather information about local celebrities. In this activity, students also learn that different criteria are used for

> **When students apply information literacy skills to issues of personal concern, they are inevitably motivated to go beyond the minimum effort needed.**

inclusion of subjects in standard resources, and must decide which resources are most likely to have what they need.

Indicator 2 for Standard 4 states that the student who is an independent learner "designs, develops, and evaluates information products and solutions related to personal interests." This indicator is closely tied to Standard 3, wherein the student "uses information effectively and creatively" in order to communicate it to others, and Standard 6, wherein the student "strives for excellence in information seeking and knowledge generation." Again, personal motivation is key to developing exemplary proficiencies. The student who is deeply involved with his subject will want to share his knowledge with others, and will attempt to demonstrate his enthusiasm for the subject as much as possible. At the most basic level, a student might present a simple cut-and-paste report, representing the bare minimum of research. The proficient student restructures the information to create a new product or a new way of looking at the information, such as in "The Exploring Three Gorges Dam" unit by Frances Campbell. This activity requires students to use a variety of search skills to find relevant information for their I-Searches about various aspects of the construction of this dam. Guidelines and rubrics keep them on task as they investigate and evaluate different kinds of resources and then combine their information into a final product.

The exemplary student "judges the quality of one's own information products and solutions." Here the student considers not just what information was found, but is also concerned with critical and creative standards for communicating and presenting this information to others. The "Going for Baroque" concert program and exhibition activity requires students to think about musical, artistic, and production elements, while being evaluated on their:

- scholarly behavior, such as demonstration of research skills, use of resources, ethical behavior, or time on task;
- aesthetic application, such as selection of music, art, and design elements in presentation and booklet, or cultural connections; and
- product completion, for example, a final concert arrangement, art display, or program booklet.

Rubrics for each element should be established by both students, teacher, and library media specialist. High expectations for exemplary products should be indicated in all of the rubrics, especially those that students have developed and will use for self-assessment.

When students apply information literacy skills to issues of personal concern, they are inevitably motivated to go beyond the minimum effort needed. And because these issues are important to them, they are more likely to assess, evaluate, and reflect on what they've learned as part of sharing that information with others. Teachers and librarians need to capitalize on this "need to know" as an ideal way to help students develop the skills they need to become life-time learners, both in and out of school.

Alice Yucht is a Teacher-Librarian at Heritage Middle School in Livingston, New Jersey.

TITLE: *Famous People from Your State or City*

AUTHORS: Mary Alice Anderson, Media Specialist, Lisa Palkowski and Barb Tibor, Teachers, Winona (Minnesota) Middle School

CURRICULUM AREAS: Social studies

CURRICULUM CONNECTIONS: Language arts

GRADE LEVELS: 5–8

PREREQUISITES:
- Basic research skills, using a variety of resources including the Internet and magazines
- Note taking and organizational skills
- Some familiarity with HyperStudio and the scanner

INFORMATION LITERACY STANDARDS FOR STUDENT LEARNING:
Standard 1, Indicator 4
Standard 3, Indicators 1, 4
Standard 4, Indicator 1

MATERIALS/SOURCES NEEDED:
- Online catalog
- Print resources on famous people from your state or city (books, pamphlets, newspaper clippings, collection of centennial issues of the local newspaper)
- Online magazine data base (Middle Search and ProQuest)
- U*X*L Biographies CD-ROM
- Web sites related to your state or city
- Biographical Web sites
- Local community Web site with information about the history of the community
- State and County historical society Web sites
- County Historical Society archives
- Guest speaker from the County Historical Society
- Scanner
- Projection system for class display
- White board and markers

STRATEGIES:

1 The teacher introduces topic as students are studying state or local history in social studies. Previously, students have become familiar with a number of possible people to study.

2 The media specialist and teacher introduces the students to a collection of newspapers commemorating the community's centennial and to state history magazines. These resources are ideal for browsing and help students decide on a topic. They are also fun to use since students get excited when seeing familiar sights or names. Students are also free to browse other resources. Students are encouraged to select a person interesting to them or related to their personal interests. Often these people are contemporary entertainers, athletes, or a community person who has contributed to the city's history. Sometimes the person may even be a relative.

3 The media specialist reviews or introduces diverse resources. The level of instruction varies with the amount of previous experience the students have and the time of year the project is completed. Questions and demonstrations revolve around an idea such as: "Let's see if the online catalog has information about _____."

4 If the person is not listed, or if there is only minimal information, the media specialist and students begin a brainstorming session to list related key words or subjects. The words are written on a white board. This question leads to questions about why there may not be books available on certain people, especially if the person is only known locally. A similar discussion is held about general encyclopedias and why they may not be a good resource for finding information about famous people from your state or city unless the person is quite significant or well known nationally.

5 What are some other resources? The media specialist introduces magazine databases. The media specialist and students brainstorm what types of people are likely to be written about in current magazines.

6 The next step is to introduce or review online biographical resources such as U*X*L Biographies, as in "What's another place we could look?" If available, another possibility for students is to introduce them to the school web site's links to biographical, state, and local information. Have a discussion about why the Internet is an ideal resource to find information about people such as athletes or entertainers who are currently popular and in the news.

7 Students begin the information gathering process. After their initial research the media specialist brings students together to answer questions and to have another discussion about why some kinds of resources are more appropriate for different categories of people. This discussion is most meaningful after students have had problems with the research process.

8 During the information-gathering process, students take notes and help each other scan pictures from books, magazines, and newspapers. They will eventually use the pictures in a HyperStudio stack. If needed, the media specialist will conduct a scanner demonstration. Make sure that the students follow the Resource Worksheet to record the sources for the information, and that they ask for permission to use photos and other pictures as needed.

9 Following the information-gathering process, students begin planning their HyperStudio stacks on HyperStudio storyboards. This usually involves more research and more scanning.

10 Students spend three to five days completing their HyperStudio stacks and two days presenting their program to classmates using a computer and video projection equipment.

11 Students could also present their HyperStudio program for County Historical Society board members and other interested community members.

EVALUATION/CRITIQUE:

The teacher and media specialist work with students throughout the information gathering and information presentation process. Student notes are checked to be sure enough information about the person has been gathered and that they have created scanned graphics of an appropriate size. HyperStudio stacks must meet prescribed criteria for content including a bibliography, color, font size, and graphics. The stack is also evaluated for technical features including buttons that work, sounds, and appropriate special effects. As students work on their stacks, they are saved on the school's server (if available) and appropriate use of the server space is considered if this is the case. If school server is not available, students should save to disks.

COMMENTS/TIPS/FOLLOW-UP:

This project can be highly successful. Students have an opportunity to learn about a person of interest to them. They enjoy accessing old newspapers and learning more about their own community. Interaction with the Historical Society and other community members who see their presentations is motivational. This activity also promotes positive school-community relations and gives library media specialists and teachers a wonderful way to showcase student research in the community.

Since this project involves a great deal of active, engaged learning, the media specialist and teacher have to be prepared to work in an often chaotic environment; accept that things will sometimes go wrong, and be prepared to provide a lot of time and space. The project can take up to three weeks.

Name: _____

Hour: _____

HYPERSTUDIO PROJECT

HYPERSTUDIO TOPIC:

BIBLIOGRAPHY

- This will be the last card of your HyperStudio program.
- You must list the resources where you found information on your topic.
- You must have at least one page of written notes.
- Pictures—if you find one, scan it into your folder
- Follow the bibliography form.

You must have one page of written notes and a bibliography by:

Name: _____

Hour: _____

RESOURCE WORKSHEET

■ I got this information from:

Bibliography format—list the information needed.

■ This is the information:

Name:_____

Date:_____

Date Due:_____

Class:_____

"FAMOUS PEOPLE" ROUGH DRAFT CARDS

Name of Person
Background color
Button design
Sound?
Graphic of state?
Your name
Date
Class
Border?

Information card
Background color
Button design
Sound?
Graphic
Border

INSTRUCTIONAL GUIDE 19

TITLE: *Going for Baroque: Concert Program and Exhibition*

AUTHOR: Alice H. Yucht, Teacher-Librarian, Heritage Middle School, Livingston, New Jersey

CURRICULUM AREA: Fine Arts

CURRICULUM CONNECTIONS: Visual and Performing Arts, European History, Technology, Music

GRADE LEVELS: 8–12

PREREQUISITES:
Research skills, including:
- search strategies for both print and electronic sources
- note-taking and citation formats

Content knowledge, including:
- major musicians and artists of the Baroque period
- identifying characteristics of Baroque music and art
- basic information about performance venues, and program booklets

INFORMATION LITERACY STANDARDS FOR STUDENT LEARNING:
Standard 4, Indicators 1, 2
Standard 8, Indicators 2, 3
Standard 9, Indicators 1–4

LEARNING EXPECTATIONS/OUTCOMES:
Students will work in teams of three to four to:
- plan a musical "concert" of three to five Baroque compositions, not to exceed two hours.
- select eight to ten examples of Baroque art to be "displayed" in the concert lobby.
- use ClarisWorks to design and produce a booklet (8–12 pages) with background information, illustrations about the music and art being showcased, and a bibliography of resources used; and design the layout of a concert hall and lobby, showing a display of artworks and other features.

MATERIALS/SOURCES NEEDED:

Students must document their use of at least two print and two electronic resource formats, for example:
- Basic and specialized reference sources on music and art of the Baroque period.
- Art and music history CD-ROMs, such as Culture 3.0.
- Music performance recordings (CD-ROMs and audio tapes)
- Bookmarked Web sites about baroque musicians, artists, orchestras, or performance venues.

STRATEGIES:

 Note: *Students are scheduled for three class periods for library research. They must then present a dummy of the final booklet before actual production in the computer lab.*

SESSION 1: Library media specialist and teacher review kinds of information needed:

■ biographical information about composers and artists

■ historical and cultural information about specific works

■ graphics and pictures for inclusion in the booklet

■ presentation details to watch for, such as length of musical piece or size of artwork

Library media specialist reviews effective search strategies for both print and electronic resources and provides brief overview of recommended resources available or bookmarked. Students begin research (making group decisions for music and art selections).

SESSION 2: The library media specialist reviews information technology ethics, citation requirements and formats, and demonstrates Copy, Cut, and Paste techniques for including graphics, such as portraits or clip art, in the program booklets. Students continue research, saving graphics to disk.

SESSION 3: Students continue research (with assistance from library media specialist or teacher as needed) and begin program booklet layout.

EVALUATION/CRITIQUE:

Students are evaluated on:

■ scholarly behavior, including demonstration of research skills, use of resources, ethical behavior, and time on task.

■ aesthetic application, including selection of music and art, design elements in presentation and booklet, and cultural connections.

■ product completion, including final concert arrangement, art display, and program booklet.

All involve both process and product and have specific time lines and rubrics generated by teachers and students.

COMMENTS/TIPS:

This kind of activity must be very carefully structured or students tend to get sidetracked. The entire project is completed in seven days: Monday-Wednesday for research, Thursday-Friday plus weekend for production, and the following Monday the completed booklet is due. This kind of schedule and pressure means that students stay focused on task and interest remains high. Working in groups with specific job responsibilities, such as music information, art information, booklet layout, artistic details, and proofreader, makes it much easier to get everything accomplished.

FOLLOW-UPS:

Although the actual concert never takes place, it does become very real to the students involved. Heated arguments about presentation set-up, sequence of musical pieces, and performance venues are common. As follow-up projects, students have suggested the following:

■ financial details, including costs of renting the hall, hiring the musicians, and promoting the event

■ reviews of the event, written for different kinds of publications or media

■ notes from composers, artists, and conductors, discussing differences in interpretation of the same theme.

TITLE: *Does It Run in the Family? Genetic Disorders*

AUTHOR: Terrence E. Young, Jr., School Library Media Specialist, West Jefferson High School, Harvey, Louisiana

CURRICULUM AREA: Science

CURRICULUM CONNECTIONS: Social Studies, Language Arts, Biology

GRADE LEVELS: 7–12

INTRODUCTION:

The primary purpose of this activity is to help students to become aware of the existence of inherited conditions and to understand that knowing about inherited conditions can be of use in making informed decisions about personal and social issues and values.

Genetic disorders can change lives. Students may be faced with a genetic disorder that will take counseling and much thought to arrive at decisions that could change their lives. Even if students are not faced with the genetic disorder directly, they may have to make decisions that affect them as taxpaying citizens. Using a wide variety of genetic-related scenarios may help them to be prepared when confronted with this type of situation.

This model can also be used to show students that genetic disorders do not discriminate against race, gender, or socioeconomic status but are directly related to DNA that has been passed down from ancestors or through mutations.

PREREQUISITES:

1 Familiarity with the structure and nature of DNA

2 Knowledge and understanding of basic genetics vocabulary and terms: *recessive, dominant, carrier, heterozygous, homozygous, inherited disorder, mutation, genes,* and *alleles*

3 Knowledge and construction of pedigree charts

4 Knowledge of how mutations can affect the physical appearance of an organism or its genetic makeup

INFORMATION LITERACY STANDARDS FOR STUDENT LEARNING:

Standard 2, Indicators: 1–4
Standard 4, Indicator 1
Standard 8, Indicators 1, 3

NATIONAL SCIENCE STANDARDS:

UNIFYING CONCEPT: evidence, models, and explanation
SCIENCE AND TECHNOLOGY: understandings about science and technology

SCIENCE AS INQUIRY: understandings about scientific inquiry
HISTORY AND NATURE OF SCIENCE: nature of scientific knowledge
SCIENCE IN PERSONAL AND SOCIAL PERSPECTIVES: personal and community health
LIFE, PHYSICAL, EARTH SCIENCES: molecular basis of heredity

MATERIALS/SOURCES NEEDED:

- Reference books
- Computers with CD-ROM drive and Internet access
- Periodical and newspaper databases and index access
- Presentation software such as PowerPoint

STRATEGIES:

1 This life skills lesson can be taught in a one- or two- week period, depending on the depth of the assignment. The prerequisite material should be mastered prior to beginning the library research phase.

2 Collaboration between the teacher and the school library media specialist is required to determine the depth of coverage of the topic and the information literacy model to be used (Eisenberg/Berkowitz: Big6 Model; Kuhthau: Information Seeking Process; Stripling/Pitts: Research Process).

3 The questions to be answered for each class can be limited depending on the learning abilities of the students. The assignment can be done individually or as a group.

4 Prior to the class visitation to the media center, the school library media specialist will:
- compile and bookmark appropriate Internet resources.
- acquire both nonfiction and fiction books related to genetic disorders.
- identify and inform both the teacher and students of the appropriate subject headings for efficient searching of the OPAC.

5 On the first library day the school library media specialist will introduce the library resources:
- online databases and indices
- reference books
- Internet access (methods and searching skills)
- appropriate computer software for both research and student presentations.

6 Students may be given the list of genetic disorders included with this lesson. After students have selected a genetic disorder to investigate, the teacher or library media specialist will brainstorm questions the students should attempt to answer through their research. Model questions for genetic disorders are:
- What is the name of the disorder?
- Are there any other names by which it is commonly known?
- What is the mode of inheritance?
- What are the features of the disorder?
- How does the disorder affect the victim?

- What causes the disorder?
- Is there a single cause for the disorder?
- What is it like to have the disorder?
- What is the disorder like externally, internally, biochemically, and psychologically?
- What problems are associated with the disorder?
- Is the disorder physically limiting?
- Is the disorder life-threatening?
- Is the disorder more commonly found in certain groups of people?
- How would you describe the disorder to someone?
- Is there any treatment?
- Can the basic defect be treated?
- Can the symptoms of the disorder be treated?
- Is there a cure for the disorder?
- Is there gene therapy for the disorder?
- Can the disorder be detected before its symptoms appear? If so, how?
- Is there any way to detect a carrier of the disorder? If so, how?
- How often does the disorder occur in the human population?
- What is the prognosis?
- Are there other problems associated with the disorder?
- What research is being done?
- Identify the chromosome responsible for the disorder.
- Describe how gene technology could be used to cure a genetic disorder.
- Locate a pedigree chart that traces the inheritance of the genetic disorder.
- Where can I find more information?
- What is the life expectancy of a person with the disorder?
- Is there a risk to expectant mothers who have the disorder?

RELATED TOPICS/SEARCHES:

1 Career Research: Who helps families cope with genetic disorders? Research the careers of genetic counselors and geneticists. Your report should include the following information:
- work performed, working conditions, hours, and earnings
- education and training, certification, professional associations or societies
- personal qualifications
- where employed, employment outlook, entry methods into the profession, and advancement
- related occupations

2 What is a typical day in the life of a genetic counselor or geneticist? Locate a genetic counselor or clinical geneticist in your area.

3 Both human gene therapy and the human genome project have received, and will continue to receive, much attention from the media. Students should be made aware of the importance of these issues in their future. Have students research these two issues, focusing on the arguments offered both for and against these projects. Conduct a class discussion on the relative merits of both positions so students will have an opportunity to engage in bio-ethical decision making.

4 Research some of the techniques of genetic counseling such as pedigrees, karyotypes, and amniocentesis.

5 Research what disorders, if any, are screened for by law in your state.

6 Students must make rational decisions in the future concerning questions of prenatal diagnosis, genetic screening and engineering, gene therapy, and many others requiring a familiarity with the principles of human genetics. Students will learn how their own views are based upon family, friends, and moral upbringing. They can then use this understanding and apply it to their interpretation of ethical issues.

7 What are the advantages and disadvantages of creating an extensive bank of criminal genomes? And, in general, should society have the right to pass legislation for people at risk of producing offspring with a genetic disorder?

8 The Health Insurance Portability and Accountability Act (Kassebaum-Kennedy Bill) was designed to ensure that when a worker left a job where he or she was enrolled in a group health insurance plan, that worker could not be denied enrollment in the new employer's group plan because of genetic information. Does an insurance company have the right to request a genetic screening of a person before selling health insurance coverage?

9 Place yourself in this scenario: Suppose you are applying for a job and your prospective employer has access to your medical records. Would an employer want to take on a long term employee at risk of developing a debilitating disease? Suppose you are applying for health insurance. If the insurer knew you were suffering from a condition that would require long-term, expensive care in the near future, would it be willing to offer you insurance? And if did offer you insurance, would it offer you a policy at a rate that you could afford?

10 Should insurance companies be entitled to access information revealed during genetic screening procedures? Should the government? Should anyone else?

EVALUATION/CRITIQUE:

- The teacher and the school library media specialist will determine if the criteria and standards were successfully met and if the information process model was followed.

- Students will be evaluated on accuracy, following directions, use of critical thinking skills, and the forming of conclusions.

- Students will submit a research paper in the format required by the teacher. The paper must include a bibliography of reference books, web sites, and electronic resources.

- Students must have answered the required questions.

- Students will present to the class a multimedia presentation that focuses on the highlights of the disorder.

SUGGESTED FICTION READING LIST:

1 Baer, Judy. *Heartless Hero*. Bethany House Publishers, 1997. 1-55661-835-2. Lexi's younger brother Ben, who has Down Syndrome, becomes the victim of bullies, and while at school Lexi sees her friends tormented by two new students who are bullies, one male and one female.

2 Deford, Frank. *Alex: Life of a Child*. Rutledge Hill Press, 1997. 1-55853-552-7. A father tells of his daughter's life with cystic fibrosis.

3 Dodds, Bill. *My Sister Annie*. Caroline House, 1993. 1-56397-114-3. Dealing with an older sister who has Down syndrome is the toughest challenge that eleven-year-old Charlie has to face.

4 McDaniel, Lurlene. *A Time To Die*. Bantam, 1992. 0-553-29809-7. Sixteen-year-old Kara doesn't know why she was born with cystic fibrosis. When an anonymous benefactor promises to grant a single wish with no strings attached, Kara can't help but wonder if miracles might really happen. Will she live to see her dying wish?

5 Perske, Robert. *Show Me No Mercy: A Compelling Story of Remarkable Courage*. Abingdon Press, 1984. 0-687-38435-4. Paralyzed in an accident that kills his wife and daughter, Any Banks, a bus driver, struggles to overcome his handicap and to keep his teenage son with Down Syndrome from being institutionalized.

6 Radley, Gail. *CF in His Corner*. Four Winds Press, 1984. 0-590-07901-8. Fifteen-year-old Jeff believes strongly that his seven-year-old brother Scotty, who suffers from cystic fibrosis, should be told the truth about his disease and his expectations for the future.

Select a genetic disorder from the list below:

Albinism
Alcoholism
Alzheimer's
Breast cancer
Burkitt lymphoma
Cleft Lip/Palate
Colorblindness
Cooley's anemia
Cri-du-chat Syndrome
Cystic Fibrosis
Diabetes insipidus
Diabetes mellitus
Down Syndrome
Duchenne Muscular Dystrophy
Edward's Syndrome/Patau's Syndrome
Epidermolysis
Familial Hypercholesterolemia
Fragile X syndrome
Galactosemia
Gaucher's disease
G6PD (Glucose 6 phosphate dehydrogenase) Deficiency

Hemophilia
Huntington's Disease
Immune deficiency diseases
(Boy in the bubble)
Klinefelter's Syndrome
Marfan Syndrome
Neurofibromatosis
Osteogenesis Imperfecta
Parkinson's disease
Phenylketonuria
Pituitary dwarfism syndrome
Polycystic kidney disease
Polydactyl
Sensorineural deafness
Sickle-Cell Anemia
Spina Bifida/Anencephaly
Tay Sachs Disease
Thalassemia
Turner's Syndrome

TITLE: *Exploring Three Gorges Dam Through I-Search*

AUTHOR: Frances Y. Bradley Campbell, Graduate Student, School of Library and Media Studies, James Madison University, Harrisonburg, Virginia

CURRICULUM AREA: Geography, Social Studies

CURRICULUM CONNECTIONS: World History, Technology, Science, Economics, Math

GRADE LEVELS: 10-12

PREREQUISITES: Brief introduction to China; introduction to or experience with searching electronic resources.

INFORMATION LITERACY STANDARDS FOR STUDENT LEARNING:
Standard 1, Indicators 3-5
Standard 2, Indicators 1-4
Standard 4, Indicator 2

OTHER OUTCOMES/STANDARDS:
I-SEARCH:
- Identify topic of interest.
- Formulate a definitive research question.
- Access, evaluate, integrate and present information answering a research question.

MATERIALS/SOURCES NEEDED:

INFORMATION RESOURCES:
- Video "Three Gorges: Biggest Dam in the World" (running time - 52 minutes) **http://shopping.discovery.com/genre/home_videosbest_sellers.html** (Item # 724195 - $19.95) Throughout its history, China has been plagued by a large, muddy, unpredictable killer: the Yangtze River. Now the Chinese have a plan to tame the river by building the monumental Three Gorges Dam. The dam will be the world's largest concrete structure. It is slated to be 650 feet high, over 2+ miles across, and will create a reservoir 400 miles long. It will use more material than 44 great pyramids, will require 2,500 people, and will cost up to $70 billion. Its hydroelectric generator will produce the equivalent of 15 nuclear reactors. Between 1.2 million and 2 million inhabitants need to be relocated. Fourteen major cities, approximately one hundred towns and more than 4,000 villages will be submerged. Cultural, historical, and religious antiquities could be lost. Endangered plants and animals may be threatened to the point of extinction. Economically, ocean freight liners will be able to sail from San Francisco into the interior of China. The massive power and scale of the dam project contrasts with the delicate landscape and human lives surrounding it.

- Print resources
- Electronic resources
- Periodical database
- Internet access

MATERIALS NEEDED:

- Television and video cassette recorder
- Overhead projector and transparencies
- Computer and ability to project for whole class viewing
- Internet resource evaluation forms (see step 3)
- Bibliographic citation forms (see step 3)
- 3-ring binder or notebook for each student

STRATEGIES:

The library media specialist and teaching team are to co-plan, co-teach, and co-evaluate the Three Gorges Dam unit following the I-Search method. Each student will:

- identify a topic of interest and develop an I-Search question to guide research.
- develop a search plan, identifying resources to be used to gather information.
- follow and revise search plan to collect, sort, and integrate information.
- prepare a paper with integrated information which may become the final product or foundation of presentation (projects).
- present or share the final product with fellow classmates.
- journal the research process (organization of material and information is essential to ensure that students do not become overwhelmed and get "off track").

The library media specialist and teaching team evaluate and approve each phase of the research process before students proceed to the next step, allowing students to feel a sense of achievement and closure throughout the process.

STEPS:

1 After viewing the video, the library media specialist or teaching team model and explain I-Search Webbing. Students then engage in and complete an individual I-Search webbing activity to identify topic of interest and develop research question. The library media specialist or teaching team assists students in the webbing activity if needed.

2 The library media specialist or Teaching Team assess and evaluate each individual student's topic of interest and research question. Determine if research question is too narrow (not searchable) or too broad (complex). Obviously, the question must be answerable. The library media specialist or teaching team sign acceptability before students begin next step.

Not Acceptable	Topic is Clear.	Question not Formulated.	
Not Acceptable	Topic is Clear.	Question is Clear.	
Acceptable	Topic is Clear.	Question is Clear.	Question is answerable.

3 The library media specialist briefly reviews school resources and research basics. Due to the currency of the unit focus, the majority of resources will be electronically based. Emphasis is placed on search engines, search syntax, and operations.

4 For example, "Finding It Online: Web Search Strategies," is HIGHLY RECOMMENDED. (**http://home.sprintmail.com/~debflanagan/main.html**) This is an interactive "hands-on" site with a tutorial presenting an easy-to-follow process on using search engines and subject directories for finding what you need on the World Wide Web. Specifically, this site will enable students to:

- use subject directories and describe the difference between a subject director and a search engine.
- use implied and full Boolean logic, phrase searching, truncation, and field searching effectively.
- identify key concepts, synonyms, and variant word forms in a search topic.
- use key search engines effectively, including Alta Vista, Infoseek, HotBot, Northern Light, Excite, and Google.
- use meta-search engines.
- use specialty databases when appropriate.

5 Student develops search plan or blueprint to identify resources using Venn diagram, Web, matrix, time line, lists, outlines, or columns.

6 Student develops search strategy using Boolean logic, phrase searching, truncation, and so on, and identifies search engines and meta-search engines to be used. The library media specialist or teaching team assess, evaluate and accept search plan before students begin the next step.

Not Acceptable	No Search Strategies		
Not Acceptable	Search Strategies		
Not Acceptable	Search Strategies	Print Resources	
Acceptable	Search Strategies	Print Resources	Electronic Resources

7 The library media specialist reviews strategies to evaluate Internet resources.

8 For example, "Kathy Schrock's Guide for Educators: Critical Evaluation Survey–Secondary School Level" is HIGHLY RECOMMENDED. (**http://discoveryschool.com/schrockguide/evalhigh.html**) Use the above form or create one. Students must learn to evaluate Web sites based upon authorship or sponsorship, purpose, bias, content, design, ease of use, and stability.

9 The library media specialist or teaching team reviews proper bibliographic citation. For example, "NUEVA Library Research Goal" is HIGHLY RECOMMENDED. (**http://www.nueva.pvt.k12.ca.us/~debbie/library/research/research.html**) The site includes MLA bibliographic Format–Interactive Forms so you can cut and paste citations into your document. Use the above site directly or create similar forms for use. Students may need forms for citing a book, e-mail message, online discussion list or forum posting,

CD-ROM, interview, magazine article, online magazine article, newspaper article, online newspaper article, professional Web page, scholarly project, or personal Web site.

10 The library media specialist or teaching team works with students to ensure proper evaluation and citation of resources (an on-going process) and assists individual students whose research plans need to be revised.

11 The library media specialist or teaching team meets with students to direct sorting and integration of information. The student then develops a rough outline with acquired information to answer the I-Search question. The library media specialist or teaching team assesses, evaluates, and approves rough outline before student begins next step.

Not Acceptable	Evaluation Forms Completed		
Not Acceptable	Evaluation Forms Completed	Bibliographic Citation Forms Completed	
Acceptable	Evaluation Forms Completed	Bibliographic Citation Forms Completed	Rough Outline With Integrated Information

Using the rough outline, students integrate information to create a paper which may become the final product or the foundation for a final product (model, graph, project, etc.). Paper must contain bibliographic citations. The library media specialist or teaching team assesses and evaluates the final product. Student will present the topic of interest and answered I-Search question to classmates.

After completion of the above steps, students should have acquired the skills to access, evaluate, integrate, and present information. Each student has completed the task in manageable formatted steps with each step providing personal achievement and closure for every student.

CHAPTER 5

Building a Reading Legacy

By Donna Miller

STANDARD 5: The student who is an independent learner is information literate and appreciates literature and other creative expressions of information.

According to *Information Power: Building Partnerships for Learning,* a student who meets Standard 5 "applies the principles of information literacy to access, evaluate, enjoy, value, and create artistic products" in all formats, including "print, nonprint, and electronic formats." This covers a broad spectrum of applications and experiences, from simply reading a book or magazine for pleasure to actually creating a sophisticated desktop publishing product. Basic levels of proficiency range from selecting books for personal reading to enjoying literature and nonfiction from various cultures, or perhaps illustrating a scene or character from a favorite book. Advanced proficiency levels include projects and activities that involve creation of more complicated products; analysis of artistic and literary works, and synthesizing knowledge by creating products or projects that integrate information or ideas learned. Thus teachers and library media specialists have wide latitude in structuring learning activities for students to enable them to meet this standard.

The three indicators for Standard 5 include three levels of proficiency: basic, proficient, and exemplary. Indicator 1 states that the student "is a competent and self-motivated reader" (*Information Power*, p. 26). It is important that teachers and library media specialists do purposeful planning to provide opportunities for junior and senior high school students to read for pleasure. All too often we see eager elementary school readers "lose the reading habit" when they move up to the next level of schooling. Booktalks and other activities that promote literature are important, but it is also important to allocate time for casual reading of books and magazines.

The "proficient" level for Indicator 1 involves students selecting reading material and "analyzing literary plots, themes, and characters" *(Information Power,* p. 26). "Using Picture Books in the Middle School" by Susan Anhold suggests that picture books can be used to introduce students to these complex concepts. As an added benefit, students (and library media specialists!) get to revisit some of their favorite books from childhood. Students create posters based on the picture books to demonstrate their understanding. Becky Mather's "Read and Rap" lesson, in which fifth grade girls are paired with a female high school reading partner, enables both the younger students and their older mentors to share their ideas and thoughts about books they read in common. This lesson addresses Standard 5, Indicator 1 with the high school students, via e-mail, asking their young friends questions to help them discuss, analyze, and choose literature as they build skills in using technology. The rubric provided by Mather completes the lesson and serves as a valuable tool for teachers and library media specialists. Assignments relevant to the "exemplary" level for Standard 5, Indicator 1 use "compare and contrast" themes in which students discuss strengths and weaknesses of literature that they have read. The emphasis of Indicator 1 is reading and analyzing literary works.

Indicator 2 for Standard 5 states that the

> **Booktalks and other activities that promote literature are important, but it is also important to allocate time for casual reading of books and magazines.**

student "derives meaning from information presented creatively in a variety of formats" (*Information Power*, p.26). This indicator takes students to a higher level of performance by concentrating on the analysis of information sources, but it includes such works as plays and "other creative presentations of information," not simply nonfiction works (*Information Power*, p. 26). At the "basic" level, students explain and discuss these works. The "proficient" level of performance adds analysis of creative works in a variety of formats. Finally, the "exemplary" level addresses evaluation of strengths and weaknesses of creative, information-based works. The primary differences between Indicator 1 and Indicator 2 are that Indicator 1 focuses on fiction and other works considered "literature" while Indicator 2 includes information-based works. Indicator 2 also emphasizes deriving meaning or analyzing works, while Indicator 1 deals more with selecting literature and demonstrating enjoyment by being an avid reader. In other words, Indicator 1 focuses on the "affective" domain of learning while Indicator 2 focuses on the "cognitive" domain.

Indicator 3 "develops creative products in a variety of formats" (*Information Power*, p. 27), addressing affective and cognitive domains. Students express information and ideas (affective) by creating products (cognitive) that take a variety of forms. At the "basic" level, students will express their ideas in simple formats such as drawings or basic stories. The "proficient" level encourages expression of information and ideas in products incorporating more than one format. Examples of this level are students writing and illustrating a story based on one they have read, or writing a play and creating a graphical billboard or advertisement for the play and skills such as editing their work, using a word processor, and reading their stories aloud to younger students. Two lessons in this chapter utilize photographs to help achieve Indicators 2 and 3. "The Faces of Child Labor" by Chris Flench draws on historic photographs taken by Lewis Hine. Through their study of these historical photographs, students are able to learn about an era and culture while also gaining valuable experience in utilizing primary sources for research. In "Photo Novella" by Lesley Farmer, students use photographs in a very different way. After studying examples of photo novellas, students choose a story they would like to tell in this format and then use a variety of technologies to create their own unique product. Both lessons show how visuals can be used to amplify and expand the power of the written word.

At the "exemplary" level students create unique products that "integrate information in a variety of formats" *(Information Power,* p. 27). For example, this could include students creating an original painting that reflects their emotions after reading a book on the Holocaust. Original songs, poetry, computer-generated games, and Internet web sites all fall in this category. Students at this level of proficiency are able to use a variety of media and select the best type for communicating their ideas and emotions. Teachers and library media specialists will be continuously challenged to help students functioning at this level continue to stretch and grow by providing ever more difficult and creative assignments.

Standard 5 provides unlimited opportunities for library media specialists to draw on their comprehensive knowledge of resources in all formats as they help teachers structure enjoyable, worthwhile experiences for students which can serve to stimulate in them a love of learning that will last throughout their lives. What a great legacy library media specialists can leave students by fostering this love of learning and reading!

Donna Miller, Media Coordinator, Mesa County Valley School District, Grand Junction, Colorado.

TITLE: *Read and Rap: Connecting Girls through Literature and Technology*

AUTHOR: Becky Mather, Quality Learning Consultant, Mississippi Bend Area Education Agency, Bettendorf, Iowa

CURRICULUM AREA: Language Arts

CURRICULUM CONNECTIONS: Information Skills

GRADE LEVELS: 5-12

PREREQUISITES: Students should have access to e-mail and possess basic usage skills in sending and receiving e-mail.

INFORMATION LITERACY STANDARDS FOR STUDENT LEARNING:
Standard 5, Indicator 1
Standard 9, Indicators 1-4

OTHER OUTCOMES/STANDARDS:
National Educational Technology Standards, Standard 4-1.
- Builds a positive mentor relationship between high school and elementary school girls
- Critically discusses literature
- Works cooperatively in a small group sharing ideas and insights
- Critiques positive roles played by women in a variety of settings
- Demonstrates efficient use of e-mail for communication
- Effectively operates a digital camera and/or scanner

MATERIALS/SOURCES NEEDED:
- Regular e-mail access for students
- Multiple copies of books
- Lists of recommended titles

STRATEGIES:

1 Read and Rap is a collaborative e-mail project in which fifth grade and high school girls are paired to read and discuss books via e-mail. The girls read a book from a recommended list prepared by district media specialists. The books feature strong female main characters, and are at an appropriate reading and interest level for the younger girls. Historical and modern fiction, science fiction and fantasy, and biographies are included.

2 After both read a book, partners discuss the book and their reactions to it via e-mail. One book usually takes four to six weeks to complete. The girls use a digital camera or a scanner and e-mail pictures of themselves to each other at the beginning of the project. The girls meet face-to-face one or more times during the school year as a group.

3 Fifth grade teachers, a high school language arts teacher, and library media specialists oversee the project at corresponding levels and evaluate.

RELATED TOPICS:
Have students search for Web sites related to their books or authors. Develop a comparable activity for boys with a somewhat different list of book titles.

EVALUATION/CRITIQUE:
Criteria for the younger girls are listed first and criteria for the older girls are in italics.

OBJECTIVE	EXEMPLARY	ACCOMPLISHED	DEVELOPED	BEGINNING
■ Build a positive mentor relationship between high school and elementary school girls. ■ Work cooperatively in a small group sharing ideas and insights.	Responds to e-mail promptly, at least three times a week. *Communicates with partner five or more times a week. Frequently initiates new ideas.*	Answers most questions soon after receiving them. *Initiates new ideas sometimes; communicates with partner three to four times a week.*	Sometimes responds to questions; may take several days. *Occasionally initiates new ideas; communicates with partner twice a week.*	Unable to respond to questions *Does not initiate new ideas; very little communication with partner.*
■ Critique positive roles played by women in a variety of settings. ■ Critically discuss literature	Offers a fair amount of information (all is relevant to discussion). *Usually initiates discussion requiring higher thinking skills.*	Most information offered is relevant to discussion. *Constructs some questions using high level thinking skills.*	Answers infrequently or with irrelevant information. *Constructs mostly low level questions.*	Rarely or never answers questions. *Constructs almost all questions at low levels of thinking skills.*
■ Demonstrate efficient use of e-mail ■ Effectively operate a digital camera and/or scanner	Uses e-mail and digital images without help to communicate with partner. *Uses e-mail and digital camera or scanner to communicate with partner; sends one or more digital photo per book*	Occasionally needs teacher's help to use e-mail and camera or scanner. *Uses e-mail and camera or scanner with occasional assistance; sends a digital photo for each session*	Frequently needs assistance using e-mail and camera or scanner. *Uses e-mail but rarely sends a digital photo to partner.*	Cannot communicate with partner without assistance. *Uses e-mail but never uses the digital camera or scanner to include a photo.*

COMMENTS:

1 The high school girls receive help from their language arts teacher on questioning techniques, for example, asking open-ended questions. This helps to break each book into sections for discussion purposes. We found that the younger girls needed to print their e-mail, then plan or write a response before sitting down at the computer. We required that each girl send a minimum of two e-mail messages per week. The girls met each other after the first book, and enjoyed seeing each other face-to-face. All the girls are volunteers and receive extra credit from their teachers.

2 Setting up meeting times during the school day (for example, during English class) fit the busier high school girls' schedules. The library media specialist arranges transportation for fifth graders, by either driving them or recruiting parent volunteers. Girls could walk (with an adult) if it's a short distance.

TITLE: *Using Picture Books in the Middle School*

AUTHOR: Susan Anhold, Graduate Student, James Madison University, Virginia

CURRICULUM AREA: Language Arts

CURRICULUM CONNECTIONS: Multidisciplinary

GRADE LEVEL: 6-8

PREREQUISITES: Fourth grade and up reading level

INFORMATION LITERACY STANDARD FOR STUDENT LEARNING:
Standard 5, Indicator 2

OTHER OUTCOMES/STANDARDS:
- Student will be able to distinguish between plot and theme.
- An understanding of the literary elements of plot and theme is made easier for the middle school student by using picture books because of their short length and simple text. This knowledge can then be transferred to identify plot and theme in a novel.
- Middle school students are missing out on some of today's wonderful "older" picture books. Many of these books have complex story lines which can be better appreciated by the older child. The pictures also enhance comprehension for the less skillful reader, which make them a valuable resource for English as a second language student. Using picture books in the classroom as a teaching tool will help spark a renewed interest in these books, lifting the stigma that picture books are just for "little kids."

MATERIALS/SOURCES NEEDED:
- A wide selection of picture storybooks with definite plots and themes (but no ABC, number, or wordless picture books; see bibliography for examples)
- Assortment of novels appropriate to the reading levels within the class

STRATEGIES:
1. To introduce the concepts of plot and theme, the teacher will lead a class discussion on what the students think these concepts are and how to distinguish between the two concepts.
2. The Library Media Specialist reads a picture storybook to the whole class. The class will determine the plot and theme of the book with help from the teacher or Library Media Specialist.
3. The Library Media Specialist divides students into groups of three or four. These groups collectively select and read a picture storybook, determining its the plot and theme.

4 The groups then act out the plot and discuss the theme with the class.

5 Next, students should individually select a new book to read and determine plot and theme by themselves. At this point, students may work on their own out of class, but the student should consult with the teacher or Library Media Specialist about the plot and theme of his or her book before advancing to the next step.

6 To show an understanding of plot and theme, students will make a poster to demonstrate these concepts of their book. An example of how the poster could look might be a picture of the theme drawn in the center with illustrations of the plot surrounding the theme.

7 Once a student has identified the plot and theme, he or she will then select a novel on his or her reading level. In a one-page paper, students will describe the plot and how it relates to the theme of the book.

RELATED TOPICS:

■ Picture storybooks can also be used for teaching other literary elements: setting, characterization, style, irony, parody, flashback, and the differences between metaphors and similes. These devices are easier to spot in picture books, because students do not get bogged down with difficult vocabulary and the short text and illustrations aid in comprehension. This knowledge can then be easily transferred to novels.

■ Use alphabet picture books for teaching theme applications or alliteration (for example, *Animalia*).

■ Story poems are an exciting way to introduce a poetry unit (for example, *Horton Hatches the Egg* by Dr. Seuss).

■ Wordless picture books can be used for creative writing. The beautiful illustrations in picture books can be used to teach various styles of art and composition as well.

■ Nonfiction picture books are particularly useful in the middle school as they present material even the weaker reader will be able to comprehend, using photos and illustrations to expand the text.

EVALUATION/CRITIQUE:

During the introduction of plot and theme, does the student:

      a. ask relevant questions?

      b. demonstrate appropriate listening skills?

      c. participate in class discussion?

For the group activity, does the student:

      a. participate in the group discussion?

      b. cooperate with fellow students in the group?

      c. recognize the plot and theme of the book?

The teacher and Library Media Specialist will circulate among the groups to observe these processes.

The student's poster should:

      a. be neat (no sloppy coloring or smudges).

      b. show the plot in a logical sequence of events using pictures.

      c. distinguish between the plot and theme.

The student's final paper should:

      a. be neatly hand-written or word-processed.

      b. describe the plot as it occurred in the book.

      c. correctly identify the theme of the book while explaining why.

      d. use correct format, capitalization, punctuation, and spelling.

      e. be clearly written and sequenced.

      f. use vocabulary which will enhance the central idea.

COMMENTS/TIPS/FOLLOW-UP:

1 A picture book is defined as a book which has pictures on each page accompanied by text. The picture itself cannot stand alone, nor can the text. (An excellent example is Rathman's *Officer Buckle and Gloria*.) Picture storybooks are those which tell an actual story with words and pictures. This would not include most number and alphabet books.

2 Be sure to include a wide variety of picture storybooks, from new books which students may have missed in grade school to old favorites, such as *Mike Mulligan and His Steam Shovel* by Burton. Students love the feeling of nostalgia the old familiar books give them. Since most middle school libraries have a limited supply of picture books, you will have to rely on borrowing from the public library and local elementary schools for your picture books.

3 Several teaching methodologies are used in this lesson. It employs four intelligences in the multiple intelligence approach (linguistic, spatial, bodily-kinesthetic, and interpersonal). Mastery learning is implied since students will not be able to go to the final step (reading the novel) until they have mastered the understanding of theme and plot using a picture storybook.

For more information on using picture books in secondary education:

Coffman, Gerry A., and Judy Jackson Spohn. (1996, Sept/Oct). From A to Z: Using alphabet books as an instructional tool with older readers. *Reading Horizons*, 37, 3-15.

Fuhler, Carol J. (1994, May). Putting poetry in its place. *Middle School Journal*, 25, 12-15.

Hall, Susan. (1990). *Using Picture Storybooks to Teach Literary Devices*: Recommended Books for Children and Young Adults. Oryx Press, Phoenix, AZ. Volumes I and II.

Karlin, Andrea R. (1994, Oct). Picture story books to use in the secondary classroom. *Journal of Reading*, 38, 158-159.

Neal, Judith C., and Kay Moore (1991/92, Dec/Jan), The Very Hungry Caterpillar meets Beowulf in secondary classrooms. *Journal of Reading*, 35, 290-295.

Richardson, Maurine V., and Margaret B. Miller. Using picture books kindergarten through high school. University of South Dakota, Vermilion, SD. (ERIC Document Reproduction Service No. ED 402-543)

Sharp, Peggy Agostino. (1984, Nov.) Teaching with picture books throughout the curriculum. *The Reading Teacher*, 38, 132-137.

Scharer, Patricia L., Donna Peters, and Barbara A. Lehman. (1995, Sept.) Lessons from grammar school: How can literature use in elementary classrooms inform middle school instruction? *Journal of Adolescent & Adult Literacy*, 39, 28-34.

Sokoloski, Carol, and Mariam Jean Dreher. (1985). Discovering picture books with intermediate grade children. In Gambrell, Linda B., ed. New Directions in Reading: Research and Practice. Maryland International Reading Association. (ERIC Document Reproduction Service No. ED 255 885), 58-66.

BIBLIOGRAPHY:

Base, Graeme. *Animalia*. Harry N. Abrams, New York. 1986.

Burton, Virginia. *Mike Mulligan and His Steam Shovel*. Houghton Mifflin, Boston. 1939.

Rathman, Peggy. *Officer Buckle and Gloria*. Putnam, New York. 1995.

Seuss, Dr. *Horton Hatches the Egg*. Random House, New York.

TITLE: *State Authors*

AUTHORS: Mary Alice Anderson, Media Specialist; and Jackie Mahlke, Teacher, Winona (Minnesota) Middle School

CURRICULUM AREA: Language arts

CURRICULUM CONNECTIONS: State History, Life Science

GRADE LEVELS: 5-8

PREREQUISITES: Basic online catalog searching, basic reference search skills, keyboarding and word processing skills, and multimedia presentation basics

INFORMATION LITERACY STANDARDS FOR STUDENT LEARNING:
Standard 1, Indicator 4
Standard 3, Indicator 4
Standard 5, Indicators 1-3

MATERIALS/SOURCES NEEDED:
- Online catalog with keywords assigned to state authors (or categories)
- Books by state authors
- Author reference books
- Online encyclopedias
- Bookmarked Web sites on authors
- School Web site with links to state author sites
- Choice of presentation tools:
  Word processing programs
  Multimedia presentation tools such as HyperStudio, PowerPoint, or ClarisWorks slide show
  Crossword puzzle programs
  Timeliner software
  Video projection system

STRATEGIES:
1 The media specialist introduces the unit to the students by giving book talks about books by state authors that represent a wide range of fiction and nonfiction, reading levels, and interest levels. Anecdotes about authors and the media specialist's own favorites help bring the books to life.

2 Following the book talks, the students receive instruction on how to find books by state authors. The level of instruction varies with the students' previous experiences in the media center. Instruction includes:

a. searching for a book by the author's name.

b. browsing through the keyword code assigned to state authors to get ideas.

c. searching for a book on a certain topic that is also by a state author.

3 Students check out and read books during the next one to two weeks.

4 The next visit to the media center includes instruction on how to find information about an author. Again, the level of instruction varies with the amount of previous experience the students have had using the school's web site and the reference section. Questions and demonstrations revolve around:

a. "The last time you were here we learned how to find a book by an author."

b. "What button on the catalog screen should I click on to find information about an author?"

c. This question leads to a discussion about the author being the subject, or in the case of an autobiography, both the subject and the author of a book. The media specialist shows the students sample materials about the author in different formats (books, pamphlets, videos).

d. Ask, "If the author isn't listed in the online catalog what are some other resources?"

e. At this time the media specialist introduces author reference books such as the Linworth Author Profile Collection or the Junior Author series. Ask, "What are some other possible sources?"

f. When students mention encyclopedias, there is a discussion about why a general encyclopedia may not be a good resource for finding information about authors unless the author is very well known.

g. So, what is another place we could look?

h. As a final resource students are introduced to the school web site and links to author information.

5 Students spend one to two class periods completing research on the authors.

6 Students present information about their book and author. This may be a word processed "report," a multimedia slide show, or a visual representation such as a timeline or poster. Students are encouraged to be creative and produce what matches their abilities and interests.

EVALUATION/CRITIQUE:

The teacher has a discussion with each student on the book they read. Students are assessed on their final presentation in a manner appropriate to the presentation medium.

COMMENTS/TIPS/FOLLOW-UP:

In Minnesota, the authors unit has been in place for over ten years and is very popular. The unit can be taught in a two-week period or expanded if the teacher wishes to have the students read multiple books. The books remain popular following the unit's conclusion. Choices range from contemporary authors, such as Gary Paulsen and Marion Dane Bauer, to classics by Laura Ingalls Wilder and Maud Hart Lovelace. Some students select books by adult authors such as Garrison Keillor. Local authors add a touch of increased interest. Occasionally local authors visit the school. Other authors come to the community as guest speakers at an annual Young Writer's Conference for area schools. Some students contact authors via letter or phone.

The books are very popular and we continually update the collection; books are always coded with a special keyword in the online catalog. Since it is not always possible to find reference or online sources on all of the authors, we maintain a file of newspaper clippings, reviews, and brochures.

As a resource-based teaching unit, the activities provide an ideal, logical way to teach a variety of information literacy skills in an integrated fashion. The unit can be correlated as an interdisciplinary unit with state history. Science students often read books with an environmental or nature theme, and many of them are by the same Minnesota authors.

ONLINE SEARCH FORM

(Use only with students who receive initial online searching instruction with this unit)

Name(s)_____ & _____ & _____

Author's last name_____Author's first name_____

List up to 5 books that the author has written.

_____complete call #_____

_____complete call #_____

_____complete call #_____

_____complete call #_____

_____complete call #_____

Content for author and book presentation:

Author's name:

Author's home city and state (or where did the author live?):

Author's birth and death date (if appropriate) or approximate dates:

Information about the book you read:

Your reaction to the book you read:

Would you recommend the book to others? Why or why not?

What are some other books the author wrote?

Bibliography of sources used for the information:

TITLE: *The Faces of Child Labor: Exploring History through Photographs*

AUTHOR: Chris Ebert Flench, Graduate Student, James Madison University, Virginia

CURRICULUM AREA: History, Social Studies

CURRICULUM CONNECTIONS: Information Skills, Language Arts, Fine Arts

GRADE LEVEL: 8-12

PREREQUISITES:
- Class has some experience using online encyclopedias.
- Class has some experience searching the Internet when bookmarked sites are provided.

INFORMATION LITERACY STANDARDS FOR STUDENT LEARNING:
Standard 2, Indicators 1-4
Standard 3, Indicator 4
Standard 5, Indicators 2,3

MATERIALS/SOURCES NEEDED:
- School and public library books, CD ROMs, classroom textbooks
- Bookmarked Internet sites (Industrial Revolution, child labor, Lewis Hine, general and American history reference)
- Copies of photographs taken by Lewis Hine during the early 1900s, available and approved for reuse by schools at the Internet site called *The History Place*:
  www.historyplace.com/unitedstates/childlabor/index.html
- Many of the same photographs found in books dedicated to the topic of child labor (see bibliography; observe the following suggestions:)
  a. Copy a separate photograph for each student plus about five extras.
  b. Choose photographs representative of the variety of jobs documented by Hine.
  c. On the backs of the pictures make notes that reflect some of the information available about each photograph (dates, locations, ages, names of children, descriptions of situations). Students will use these notes as clues when they begin their research.
- Overhead transparencies of two or three other photographs by Hine; coordinate these with related narrative quotes about children at work in industry during the early 1900s (see bibliography)
- Copies of handout
- Large flip chart or bulletin board paper

■ Overhead projector

■ Project notebook for each student

STRATEGIES:

1 This unit reflects constructivist understanding of learning, emphasizing the use of primary sources (photographs) to foster interest and development of historical research. Learning takes place on two levels: individuals research specific questions of personal interest, and the group constructs an ever-expanding chart of what they are discovering about the topic.

2 Collaboration between the American History teacher and the Library Media Specialist includes meeting to share each other's expertise in content area and process, becoming familiar with some of the more specific information for this project, and planning together. As the project gets underway, both instructors should take advantage of the opportunities offered by students' reflective journals to understand the needs of students and adjust plans accordingly.

STEPS:
Day 1
OVERVIEW:

1 Class explores what they know about the topic.

2 Reflective journal entries give a baseline of individual's knowledge

3 Introduce observation and inference methods for analyzing historical photographs (see Handout A).

4 Group begins to construct chart about child labor in the early twentieth century.

SUGGESTED ACTIVITIES: WHAT WE KNOW

5 Brainstorm a list of modern-day activities students engage in on a regular basis and analyze the list for most prevalent activities. Explore the interest and experience of students in holding jobs, what they know about laws that limit the ages of child workers, the nature of the work they may do, and the hours they may work.

6 Introduce project notebooks. Ask each student to write a thoughtful entry describing what they know about the activities of children 100 years ago.

7 Display overhead transparencies of children at work while sharing quotes from the early twentieth century (see bibliography). Choose one for modeling procedures for studying historical photographs. Use Handout (Steps 1 and 2) as a guide. Have students do the same with photographs and copies of handouts for use by individuals.

8 Reassemble group to discuss their findings and record ideas on a Child Labor Chart. This will be most useful if organized from the beginning by general categories. Students will be adding ideas to this large chart each day.

Day 2
OVERVIEW:

1 Form questions about historical photographs and consider sources that would help in finding answers (see Handout).

2 Class brainstorms resources, keywords.

3 Research begins. Note-taking guidelines increase critical analysis of sources and information gathering.

4 Make changes or additions to Child Labor Chart in class meeting.

5 Reflective journal entry describes process and identifies difficulties.

SUGGESTED ACTIVITIES: WHAT WE WANT TO KNOW

6 Discuss the kinds of questions that might arise out of the study of historical photography. Some questions are simply answered (What kind of factory is this?) while others will involve complicated issues with difficult answers (What were the differences between the North and South in using children as laborers in this time period?). Allow students time to study the pictures again and complete Handout, listing both the simple and more complicated questions that come to mind (Step 3).

7 Brainstorm a list of resources that might be used to learn more about this topic and keywords that would lead to relevant information. Project notebooks should be used to record lists of keywords and phrases as they are suggested by classmates. Students should continue to add new keywords to their search lists suggesting the paths they took as they researched their questions.

8 Create a section in notebooks for keeping research notes. Suggest a system for keeping notes along with reflective analysis of what was found (left pages for notes, right pages for responses, for example). Students should consider some of the following questions in their analyses:

How does this idea fit with the information I have been reading?

How does it fit with what I know?

What about this information is confusing or seems incorrect?

If this is true, how does it answer my question?

What is the source of this information? (bibliographical reference)

9 Students begin to search for general information using Handout and their lists of keywords.

10 Near the end of the period gather again as a group. Focus each class meeting on enriching the group's understanding of the topic through the discoveries of individuals. Ask, "What did you discover that agrees with the observations we made from the photographs? Where did you find this? What did you discover that disagrees with our observations? Where did you find this?" Add new information to the chart as it is offered. "What new questions does this information suggest?"

ASSIGNMENT:

- Formulate a question about this topic that you would like to research. Questions need to represent deep thinking about the topic, and have the possibility of multiple or complex answers.

- Write reflections about today's activities. Include things you expected to find easily, problems you ran into, plans for continuing work next time, and interesting questions that came up in class discussion. Suggest resources that are needed and not available.

Search Days
OVERVIEW:

1 Students uncover new information that confirms or contradicts what the class believes to be true.

2 Group meetings elicit high quality discussions of information being discovered by individuals. Child Labor Chart grows and becomes a record of the learning taking place.

3 Individual project notebooks record progress in discovering resources, selecting pertinent information related to search questions, and analyzing each student's work.

4 Group begins to plan ways to share their learning with others.

SUGGESTED ACTIVITIES:

5 Allow time to work on research and then gather to add to the Child Labor Chart. As this builds it should reflect a growing knowledge base and information that both supports and contradicts information found by others. Class should exhibit a growing awareness that historians often generalize about events that are more complex than first thought.

6 Instructors assess students' progress, use of time and need for extra visits to the library.

7 Begin to discuss formats that would be effective vehicles for sharing research with others. One possibility would be a Museum of Child Labor with displays from each student. Displays might include relevant documents, photographs, artifacts, demonstrations, debates between conflicting parties.

8 Plan deadlines for research and projects based on the progress in class and understanding of student needs as expressed in project notebooks.

Wrapping Up
OVERVIEW:

1 Final journal entry reflects on the process from beginning to end.

2 Class shares information with another interested group.

SUGGESTED ACTIVITIES: WHAT WE LEARNED

3 When the project nears an end, a final entry in project notebooks should be a thoughtful reflection on what has been learned. This could include learning about research methods as well as specific details about child labor. Before beginning to write students should review their notebooks, look over the class chart, and revisit projects that have been presented.

EVALUATION/CRITIQUE:

1 Assessment of project notebooks is ongoing and critical to understanding the ability of each student to research this topic. The first two entries should be read and discussed by both instructors, while later entries can be observed less frequently (every third day). Notebooks should include required elements (handout, updated keyword list, research notes and reflections.)

2 Notes should go beyond simple fact-grabbing, and should reflect a student's ability to evaluate usefulness of information to their quest.

3 Reflection entries should be thoughtful, detailed, show progress in research and a developing understanding of the topic. A comparison of the first (What I Know) and last (What I Learned) entries ought to make it clear to teacher and student how much was accomplished.

4 Project evaluation should reflect significant historical content and each student's ability to relate historical information to others in an accurate, effective, and creative way.

COMMENTS/TIPS/FOLLOW-UP:

The success of this unit will depend in great measure on the preparation of the library media specialist and history teacher. The library media center needs to provide access to an adequate number of resources so that every student can be fully engaged in research. The following bibliography of books and Internet sites may be useful in beginning to collect resources.

BIBLIOGRAPHY:
ABOUT LEWIS HINE:

Freedman, Russell. *Kids at Work: Lewis Hine and the Crusade Against Child Labor.* Clarion, 1994, 104 pp.

Curtis, Verna Posever, and Stanley Mallach. *Photography and Reform: Lewis Hine and the National Child Labor Committee.* Milwaukee Art Museum, 1984.

Kaplan, Daile, ed. *Photo Story: Selected Letters and Photographs of Lewis W. Hine.* Smithsonian Institution Press, 1992.

America and Lewis Hine: A film by Nina Rosenblum and Daniel V. Allentuck. New York: The Cinema Guild, 1984.

ABOUT CHILD LABOR:

Trattner, Walter I. *Crusade for the Children: A History of the National Child Labor Committee and Child Labor Reform in America.* Quadrangel Books, 1970.

Currie, Stephen. *We Have Marched Together: The Working Children's Crusade.* Lerner, 1997, 88 pp.

Stein, R. Conrad. Cornerstones of Freedom: *The Story of Child Labor Laws.* Childrens Press, 1984, 31 pp.

Hakim, Joy. A History of US: Book 5: *Liberty for All?* Oxford University Press, 1994, 192 pp.

Meltzer, Milton. *Cheap Raw Material: How our Youngest Workers are Exploited and Abused.* Viking, 1994, 167 pp.

Greene, Laura Offenhart. *Child Labor: Then and Now.* Franklin Watts, 1992, 144 pp.

Freedman, Russell. *Immigrant Kids.* Dutton, 1980, 72 pp.

Seeger, Pete and Bob Reiser. *Carry it On! A History in Song and Picture of the Working Men and Women of America.* Simon and Schuster, 1985, 256 pp.

INTERNET SITES:

National Child Labor Committee Collection
http://lcweb.loc.gov/rr/print/207_hine.html

Children for Hire: Child Labor in the U.S. Today
http://www.nando.net/nt/special/morechildren.html

IRWeb: Information Page
http://tqjunior.advanced.org/4132/info.htm

Mr. Coal's Story: Child Labor Bulletin
http://www.history.ohio-state.edu/projects/childlabor/mrcoalsstory/

The Story of My Cotton Dress: Child Labor Bulletin, August 1914
http://www.history.ohio-state.edu/projects/childlabor/cottondress/

Between a Rock and a Hard Place: A History of American Sweatshops
http://www.si.edu/organiza/museums/nmah/ve/sweatshops/history/1880.htm

The History Channel: Child Labor
http://www.historychannel.com/cgi-bin/framed.cgi

National Archives and Records Administration: Primary Sources and Activities
http://www.nara.gov/education/teaching/teaching.html

UNCOVERING THE STORIES
BEHIND HISTORICAL PHOTOGRAPHS

STEP 1. OBSERVATION:

Study the photograph for 2 minutes. First try to get an idea of the WHOLE picture, then look for small details. Next, divide the photo into four sections and study each smaller part to see what new details become visible.

A Use the chart below to list people, objects and activities in the photograph.

PEOPLE	OBJECTS	ACTIVITIES

B What information has been added to the photograph? Be sure to inspect the back for handwritten notes.

_____

_____

_____

STEP 2. INFERENCE:

Based on what you have observed above, list three things you can say might be true about this period of history, its children, and work.

_____

_____

_____

STEP 3. QUESTIONS:

A What questions does this photograph raise in your mind?

_____

_____

_____

B Where could you find answers to them?

_____

_____

_____

Adapted from Photograph Analysis Worksheet originally designed and developed by the Education Staff,
National Archives and Records Administration, Washington, DC 20408 (http://www.nara.gov/education/teaching/analysis/photo.html)

TITLE: *Photo Novella*

AUTHOR: Lesley S. J. Farmer, Associate Professor, California State University, Long Beach

CURRICULUM AREA: Language Arts

CURRICULUM CONNECTIONS: Foreign Languages, Social Studies, Fine Arts

PREREQUISITE: Basic visual literacy; storyboarding experience (optional)

GRADE LEVELS: 9-12

INFORMATION LITERACY STANDARDS FOR STUDENT LEARNING:
Standard 2, Indicator 4
Standard 3, Indicators 1, 4
Standard 5, Indicators 2, 3

OTHER OUTCOMES/STANDARDS:
BIG6: Task Definition/Identify information needed
■ Students will be able to identify information needed to create a photo novella.

Use of Information/Extract relevant information
■ Students will be able to determine which images best explain an idea.

Synthesis/ organize information from multiple sources, present the information
■ Students will be able to sequence visuals logically.
■ Students will be able to link visual and written information.
■ Students will be able to create a photo novella.

MATERIALS/SOURCES NEEDED:
■ Photos or other visual materials
■ Supplies for creating a photo novella (such as paper, writing tools, glue)

STRATEGIES:

1 Library Media Specialist shows class a photo novella and discusses its elements, benefits, and possible uses.

2 The class may compare photo novellas to comic books.

3 Library Media Specialist or content teacher discusses visual literacy elements and how visuals can be used to explain an idea.

4 Library Media Specialist or content teacher explains how to caption visuals, balancing visual and written information.

STEPS:

1 Students choose a story or process to explain (such as how to get a passport, how to obtain bank account, how to wash a baby).

2 Students storyboard their topic.

3 Students locate or create visuals to illustrate the story or process.

4 Students sequence visual elements.

5 Students write captions for each visual.

6 Students produce finished photo novella.

WRAP UP:

■ Students compare photo novellas, and discuss the use of visual and written information in telling a story or explaining a process. They may want to compare photo novellas to other visual presentation forms, such as comic books, film, Lego instructions.

■ Students may explore how other cultures use photo novellas and graphic novels (Japan and Europe in particular).

EVALUATION/CRITIQUE:

Students evaluate their peers' photo novellas in terms of clarity, logical, sequencing, accuracy, thoroughness, and technical quality.

COMMENTS/TIPS/FOLLOW UP:

1 Photo novellas (sophisticated comic books) are used and highly valued in Latino countries, Japan, Europe, and especially France. This activity enables students to see these sequential visual documents in a new light, as well as learn to coordinate written and visual information.

2 Students may need help doing storyboards.

3 Students may use graphic software to edit or import photos and add text. They may create a multimedia photo novella.

4 Students may create rubrics (or use an existing one) to guide and evaluate their work. If students are not accustomed to using rubrics, additional time should be taken.

BIBLIOGRAPHY OF ELECTRONIC SOURCES:

http://isurf.yahoo.com is a good search engine for images.

The keyword "anime" links to Japanese animation, which is related to graphic novels.

CHAPTER 6

Striving for Excellence

By Shayne Russell

STANDARD 6: The student who is an independent learner is information literate and strives for excellence in information seeking and knowledge generation.

A s we become acquainted with the new information literacy standards introduced in *Information Power: Building Partnerships for Learning*, no doubt we are each looking for our own definition of what these standards will look like in our own media centers. As I read through the activities selected to represent Standard 6, a common thread emerged, which for me is the concept that defines the standard, that of evaluation.

Generally viewed by students as something that happens after a project is completed, evaluation is an ongoing process, as Standard 6 reminds us, this is the role played as a Library Media Specialist in planning and preparation. "Excellence in information seeking" starts with an evaluative process in which students think about their

topic, generate questions, and then think some more in order to focus their search in a well-defined direction that will uncover answers worth knowing. "Exploring Career Options," "Exploring Historical Resumés," and "Thoreauing" all guide students in this important definition of topic. Evaluation extends beyond the development of the topic to the thoughtful appraisal of available resources.

"Thoreauing" by Victoria Santucci requires students to discriminate between relevant, credible, supporting material and that which is poorly researched. In this lesson, students are asked to apply what they have learned about Thoreau's philosophy to current social problems. As a group, students must research a current social problem, then present a creative solution in a nontraditional format, such as a collage or PowerPoint presentation. The cooperating teacher and library media specialist evaluate students based on both individual contributions to the final project and the final project as a whole. Suggestions for providing feedback throughout the process are included to help ensure students are making satisfactory progress. It's refreshing that the activities in this chapter share a view of evaluation as a self-determining one as opposed to something we "do to" students.

How will their work measure up? What of "excellence in knowledge generation"? Each of these activities culminates with an end product that will be unique to the group that created it. Each encourages students to find relevant facts and to apply them to a new situation, to incorporate them in a new creation, to generate a solution, or to support a decision. By doing so, each discourages plagiarism and increases the likelihood that students will indeed generate knowledge and understanding.

Excellence in information seeking and knowledge generation: can this really happen in your media center? You know what? It already does. Consult with your students. I asked a group of middle school boys who come in to pore over computer game magazines if they could help me figure out what would be a good computer game to buy. They began by helping to define the topic, starting with what is meant by *good*. "If you like strategy games and there's one that you like, you could buy its sequel," one boy suggested. "You can tell which games are the most popular by looking at their packages to see if they were named Game of the Year or if they've sold over a million copies," another recommended. Qualities that might define *good* for me were identified: "Are graphics important to you?" they asked. Then they considered and debated

a number of possible resources where I could continue my research.

I learned that I could go to a certain store and ask to try a game before I purchased it. I could ask the people who work in the store for recommendations. They showed me two magazines and three Web sites and patiently explained where to look and what to look for. I learned to read reviews, check for overall ratings, and where to look for announcements of new releases.

"What if I bought a game and then didn't like it?" I asked. I was informed which store in our area has the best return policy! These kids knew their stuff! If Standard 6 is defined by evaluative strategies and self-generated knowledge, these kids are there. They were knowledgeable, they were articulate, they were enthusiastic. Why hadn't I ever noticed this in class?

Upon reflection, this brings me to another key element which is shared by the Standard 6 activities you are about to read/relevance. Two of the lessons focus on a topic that students at this age find especially relevant, that is, selecting a career. "Exploring Career Options" by Mary Alice Anderson, Greg Wing, Bob Urness, Rod Schwartz, and Matt Smith is a complete career unit, taking students from self-assessment of interests through the educational requirements and future trends for a specific career choice. The authors of this lesson point out that this is an excellent example of a life-long learning activity that allows students to see the range of information resources (including human resources) that are available today. Elizabeth Bowen's "Historical Resumés" provides a model for investigating details about the lives of famous people who lived during the twentieth century. Students will have to locate information beyond what is found in textbooks,

> ## Excellence in information seeking and knowledge generation—Can this really happen in your media center? You know what? It already does.

including details about the person's hobbies, civic involvement, awards, and honors. The self-assessment included with this project requires students to reflect about the process and their product.

Students are transformed when they are dealing with something they care about or which has a real-life application. Our students can become independent learners and achieve excellence in information seeking and knowledge generation. I hope the activities in this chapter will serve as models to help set this process in motion in your media center.

Shayne Russell, Educational Media Specialist, Mt. Laurel (New Jersey) Hartford School

TITLE: *Exploring Career Options*

AUTHORS: Mary Alice Anderson, Library Media Specialist; Greg Wing, Bob Urness, Rod Schwarz, Matt Smith, Teachers; Winona (Minnesota) Middle School

CURRICULUM AREAS: Social studies

CURRICULUM CONNECTIONS: Math, Economics

GRADE LEVELS: 7-9

PREREQUISITES: self-assessment skills, Internet navigation and search skills, basic spreadsheet/graph abilities, note taking, organization, and word processing

INFORMATION LITERACY STANDARDS FOR STUDENT LEARNING:
Standard 4, Indicator 1
Standard 6, Indicator 1

MATERIALS/SOURCES NEEDED:

- Self-assessment tools provided by the teachers
- Folders for portfolios
- Spreadsheet and graphing program such as MicrosoftWorks, AppleWorks, or Excel
- Career center materials in the media center
- Web sites including career links (**http://wms.luminet.net/curricsites/index.html**)
- *Middle Search* and *Pro Quest* periodical databases
- Online or CD-ROM encyclopedia
- Encyclopedia of Careers and Vocational Guidance, CD-ROM
- Career Winds database on the school's network (desirable)
- Projection system for demonstration

STRATEGIES/STUDENT TASKS:

1 Students complete a self-assessment to help them identify interests, skills, long and short term goals. Following the self-assessment they will categorize themselves as doers, thinkers, creators, helpers, persuaders, or organizers. The class will collect data on the numbers of students who have put themselves in each of the categories.

2 After students collect data about themselves, they will enter it in a simple spreadsheet and make a pie chart. The Library Media Specialist will provide directions for those students who need a review or additional assistance. Students may choose to make the chart and graph without a computer.

3 The Library Media Specialist will introduce the students to the career center and its resources. The Library Media Specialist will discuss which types of resources may be best for certain information needs. Demonstrations will be given for:

a. accessing online databases.

b. appropriate Internet search engines and strategies.

c. finding current information in magazines (online or print copy).

d. brainstorming key search terms.

4 Students will spend three to four 50-minute class periods searching for information in multiple resources. Questions to answer include:

a. how people prepare for a career.

b. duties and responsibilities involved.

c. how the chosen career affects personal, family and community life.

d. future possibilities for work in this area.

5 Students will practice word processing and paper and pencil note-taking skills and store their information in their portfolios or on disks. Students will also use this time to locate community resources that may be of assistance. As students complete the data-gathering process, they will begin preparing for their oral presentation.

6 The students will give an oral presentation to their class. The presentation must include information about each of the questions they researched and may use a visual. The Library Media Specialist may be asked to provide assistance to students who prepare multimedia slide shows and need presentation equipment if the classroom does not have it.

EVALUATION/CRITIQUE:

Throughout the process, students and their teacher each complete a feedback checklist aligned to the task and content outcomes. Overall comments are provided by each. The feedback checklist items are:

TEACHER		STUDENT
	The self-assessment sheets clearly identify the student's skills, abilities, and personality.	
	The data collected presents a comprehensive body of information.	
	The information is clearly documented and organized.	
	The sources are sufficiently varied to provide a full and realistic view of the career options.	
	Presentation provides current, accurate information about the career option.	
	Identifies specific skills and abilities required for work in the career.	
	Provides concrete information regarding preparation for the career.	
	Provides focused suggestions for goal-setting related to the career.	
	Incorporates first-hand accounts of ways the career might impact personal, family, and community life.	

COMMENTS/TIPS/FOLLOW-UP:

Our students complete the career exploration activities as part of a Minnesota Graduation Standard on decision making. Each student receives an extensive packet of information explaining the required outcomes and tasks. Teachers use checklists to track what their students know or can do (previous knowledge) and what they need to teach. The feedback process is time-consuming, but it helps the students stay on task and organized throughout the extensive process.

The full project takes at least two weeks but can be modified to meet the abilities and needs of the students. Available physical, community, and human resources need to be considered. Exploring Career Options can be used in any career unit or life-long learning activity; it is an example of how individuals or an entire community can be a resource.

The Library Media Specialist will need to be certain that career materials are current and diverse, that web links are up to date and that students have access to phone and fax for making community contacts. Students will want to use the Internet, but should also be directed towards other current sources that will help them quickly locate developmentally appropriate information.

TITLE: *Historical Resumés*

AUTHOR: Elizabeth W. Bowen, Potomac Senior High School, Dumfries, Virginia

CURRICULUM AREA: United States History

GRADE LEVELS: 9-12

CURRICULUM CONNECTIONS: Social Studies, Information Skills, Career Exploration

OVERVIEW: Students will learn how to use CD-ROM encyclopedias while creating a resume for a twentieth century historical figure.

PREREQUISITES: Experience with computer skills such as using the mouse to navigate, and keyboarding. Students should be familiar with Big6 search method.

INFORMATION LITERACY STANDARDS FOR STUDENT LEARNING:
Standard 1, Indicators 1, 3, 5
Standard 3, Indicators 1, 3, 4
Standard 6, Indicators 1, 2

MATERIAL/SOURCES NEEDED:
- Overhead projector
- Transparencies
- CD-ROM Encyclopedias
- Computer with ability to project for whole class viewing.
- Computers for class usage

INSTRUCTIONAL ROLES:
This activity requires two or more sessions and is a cooperative project between the teacher and library media specialist. The classroom teacher will introduce the concept of resumés and review historical figures from the twentieth century. The library media specialist will introduce students to the CD-ROM encyclopedias and guide the class through a search.

STRATEGIES:

1 The teacher will introduce the concept of resumés. Students will view several different types of resumés and discuss their purpose. The teacher will brainstorm with students for names of historical figures from the twentieth century. The students will select a name from this list or propose an alternative to use for their project.

2 The library media specialist will use the computer/television or the computer/visual display to demonstrate the uses of the CD-ROM encyclopedias. At the end of the presentation, students will complete a guided search using the CD-ROM encyclopedias. The library media specialist will have students conduct a search using a historical figure from the nineteenth century, such as John D. Rockefeller.

3 After locating the information about the nineteenth-century historical figure, the teacher guides students through a resume using the overhead. At this point students will begin their independent projects.

STEPS:

1 Following a general introduction to resumés and their importance, students will receive a project guide. The teacher will discuss the guide with the class and answer any questions.

2 Each student will choose a historical figure from the twentieth century.

3 The library media specialist will teach the class how to use the CD-ROM encyclopedias, following the Big6 research strategy. The library media specialist will focus on the following:

a. typing in key word searches.

b. locating all of the relevant articles.

c. skimming to identify the main topics covered in the articles and find the sections most likely to contain needed information.

d. reading the sections that are most relevant.

e. identifying the information needed to complete the project.

4 After completing the instructional part of the lesson, the library media specialist will guide students through a search on John D. Rockefeller. The students will execute the search at the computer stations.

5 The students will use the information found on John D. Rockefeller to complete a model historical resumé with the teacher.

6 The students will begin to fill out the Search Worksheets for their independent projects. During this process, the library media specialist will check the Search Worksheets and offer suggestions and feedback.

EVALUATION/CRITIQUE:

■ The evaluation process will include input from both the library media specialist and the classroom teacher.

■ The evaluation process will include the progress made during the project such as completion of Search Worksheet, rough drafts, and peer evaluation.

■ The student will participate in the evaluation process by completing a self-assessment sheet.

■ The library media specialist will evaluate the Search Worksheet for accurate information as well as student progress in using CD-ROM encyclopedias to access information.

■ The classroom teacher will evaluate the resumé using a rubric and incorporate the student self-assessment in the final grade.

COMMENTS/TIPS/FOLLOW-UP:

- Students can be put into pairs for this project if there are not enough computers or CD ROM encyclopedias.
- Encourage students to choose someone of interest.
- Provide a diverse list of historical figures, including figures from different cultural backgrounds and figures representing both genders.
- Invite the Career Counselor to speak to your class on the various uses of resumés.
- Have students find job descriptions from the newspaper that their historical figure would be qualified for and hold a mock interview.
- Have students write job descriptions based on a historical resumé produced by the class.
- Have students role-play their historical figure in a talk-show format.
- This activity could be used across the curriculum for any biographical activity.

HISTORICAL RESUMÉS

This project for United States History will require students to compose a resumé for a historical figure from the twentieth century. It will require students to research their historical figure using CD-ROM encyclopedias.

The resume will be typed on actual resumé quality bond paper (as provided by the teacher) and must be in a standard resumé form. See the examples provided on the project board. The following are categories that should be included in the resumé:

■ **PERSONAL INFORMATION:** name, address, birthday, marital status, children

■ **EDUCATIONAL BACKGROUND:** type and amount of education or training, school name(s), degrees held, major or minor areas of study

■ **PROFESSIONAL EXPERIENCE:** employment history, employers' names, locations, years of employment, and job descriptions

■ **MILITARY SERVICE:** type of military experience, training, and number of years of service

■ **HOBBIES AND INTEREST:** things enjoyed doing outside of work; activities in which involved; hobbies in which talented or skilled

■ **CIVIC INVOLVEMENT:** type of community service, volunteer work, or charitable service

■ **ACCOMPLISHMENTS:** special successes

■ **AWARDS AND HONORS:** awards and honors received for achievement – scholastic, athletic, humanitarian, military; abilities, character, and work ethics

RESUMÉ RUBRIC

6 EXCEPTIONAL RESUMÉ:

Resumé is truly outstanding; shows great care, time and pride; demonstrates information and research outside of class and "home"; has all required categories; includes one or more extra "effects" such as a cover letter or questions; is edited for spelling and grammar; is beautifully typed on professional bond; definitely demonstrates knowledge of historical figure; is turned in on time.

5 STRONG RESUMÉ:

Resumé is excellent and shows care and pride; has all required categories; has been edited for spelling and grammar; demonstrates time spent and knowledge of historical figure; is neatly typed on bond and is turned in on time.

4 CAPABLE RESUMÉ:

Resumé meets all the requirements; includes all required categories; is neatly typed with some attention to grammar and spelling; demonstrates some time spent and knowledge of historical figure; is of average length and is turned in on time.

3 LIMITED RESUMÉ:

Resumé meets most of the requirements; is typed on bond; may or may not be turned in on time; demonstrates limited knowledge of historical figure.

2 UNACCEPTABLE RESUMÉ:

Resumé is unacceptable in that it meets too few of the requirements and needs to be revised to be given a grade.

STUDENT SELF-ASSESSMENT

Name:_____   Project:_____

(Please describe your project)

In order to complete my project I used:

The thing I enjoyed the most about doing this project was:

The thing I liked the least about doing this project was:

When I look at this project, I would improve:

One thing I think you should know about my project is:

The advice I would give a student doing this project next year is:

I would score my project a _____ because:

Teacher Evaluation_____

Comments:

TITLE: *Thoreauing*

AUTHOR: Victoria Santucci, Sherando High School, Stephens City, Virginia

CURRICULUM AREA: Language Arts

CURRICULUM CONNECTIONS: Social studies, English, Sociology

GRADE LEVEL: 11

PREREQUISITES:
Students have been studying R. W. Emerson and H. D Thoreau, Transcendentalism, social responsibility, and individualism. Students have read *The Crucible, The Scarlet Letter*, "Self-Reliance," "The American Scholar," "Civil Disobedience," and *The Night Thoreau Spent in Jail.*

INFORMATION LITERACY STANDARDS FOR STUDENT LEARNING:
Standard 6, Indicators 1, 2
Standard 7, Indicators 1, 2
Standard 9, Indicators 1-4

INTRODUCTION:
Students should come to a consensus on the philosophy behind Thoreau's ideas of independent thinking and individualism plus the need for social awareness, whether it be local, national, or global. Creating a central theme for their topics will enable them to gather the needed information and to limit, identify, and address a specific social problem.

OTHER OUTCOMES:
■ Students will develop the skills for gathering, identifying, and limiting information relevant to specific social problems they wish to address.
■ Students will learn to determine accuracy of information gathered and become more efficient in use of information resources, both printed and electronic.
■ Students will learn to keep information organized in group folders and be able to show work in progress. All students within each group must write about their contribution to the project.
■ Students will learn to evaluate and finalize their projects by stating the question or problem they are researching, showing examples, and proposing a reasonable solution supported by the information they have gathered.
■ As students develop their skills as critical thinkers and become more socially aware, they will learn to discriminate between relevant, credible, supporting material as compared to poorly researched sources.

- Students will learn to research and investigate a question or problem which interests them and retain the skills learned for future use.
- Students will become more aware of available technology for researching any topic.

MATERIALS/SOURCES NEEDED:

- Notes from class
- Access to Internet
- Print resources
- Electronic resources
- Construction paper, paste
- Colored pencils, colored markers
- Colored poster boards, folders
- Pictures from printed resources
- Overhead projector
- SIRS Researcher, PowerPoint, or other presentation software

STRATEGIES:

1 Teacher leads discussion on Thoreau's philosophy in the classroom to determine meaning behind independent thinking, individualism, and social awareness.

2 In the classroom, teacher and students brainstorm the many social problems in our world. Each student writes about what has been discussed in class, making reference to a particular social problem which interests them and where they stand on the issue (this will help the teacher in assigning study groups).

3 Students meet in small groups (no more than four to a group). Teacher will provide each group with a folder into which all information will be gathered. The information in the folders is used by the teacher and Library Media Specialist to monitor the group's progress and to insure that everyone in the group is participating appropriately.

4 Using notes from previous class, groups discuss and choose one topic and theme they feel strongly about for their project. Everyone in the group writes their own paragraphs on why they have chosen their topic and how they plan to approach it. All notes can be kept in group folder for future reference. Teacher and Library Media Specialist can review notes to follow what students are doing and for future comments.

5 FIRST ROUGH DRAFT: Each group hands in one page, including a written explanation about ideas on their topics. Topics must be defined, and group must state direction planned for researching topics. All written information goes into group folder for teacher and Library Media Specialist to review.

6 After groups decide what they want to research, the teacher and Library Media Specialist meet with students to discuss their projects (in classroom or library).

7 In the classroom all students in each group write how they perceived the discussion went with the Library Media Specialist and how collaboration between students and the Library Media Specialist can be approached. All notes go into the folder for teacher and Library Media Specialist to review.

8 Students go to library media center. The library media specialist is "armed" with each group's folders, and is ready to discuss and demonstrate how to best gather information using different print materials and other resources. Boolean search method, use of CD-ROMS, and selection of an Internet search engine may be reviewed depending on each group's area of interest and expertise with technology. Small or large group instruction may be required.

9 Library Media Specialist and students will discuss how best to present each group's final project: collage, music, overhead, or slides.

10 SECOND ROUGH DRAFT: Groups will outline topics to be addressed in the final project. Topics are defined using relevant information about the problem, its geographical location, its social and political significance. The proposed solution is also addressed. If content and format is acceptable to both the teacher and Library Media Specialist, students proceed to the next step. If not, the group must retrace their steps and reformulate from their first rough draft (step 5).

11 Each student prepares his or her individual contribution to the final project, using format selected by the group. The group meets and students collaboratively assemble the components into the finished, final project.

12 Students present project to the entire class (each group member presents some part of the project to teacher and Library Media Specialist) and display projects (that can be displayed) in the library media center.

EVALUATION:

- Participation in brainstorming class discussion (teacher)
- Clearly written, individual rational response on choice of topic (Library Media Specialist and teacher)
- Group cooperation and constructive collaboration with Library Media Specialist (Library Media Specialist)
- Folders turned in after every class with written responses by each student in the group which shows progress in discussion of topic (Library Media Specialist and teacher)

First written rough draft of topic by group (step 5)

- Demonstrates understanding of social problem (teacher)
- Theme of project is obvious and complexity of problem is apparent. (teacher)

Library visits

- Library work is documented in group folders and shows progress of group work. (Library Media Specialist)
- Students are using print material and analyzing material relevant to topic. (Library Media Specialist)
- Students document and interpret how print or technology sources will be used.
- Information is put into group's folders for teacher and Library Media Specialist to review.

Second rough draft (step 10)

- Demonstrates logical organization and realistic understanding of problem
- Demonstrates depth/insight into definition of topic
- Shows relationship of problem to society, whether national or global

Final presentation of project

- Each group member presents a part of the project to demonstrate his or her skills in speaking and the use of diverse and creative modes of presentation.
- Each group member can define clearly what topic is being presented and what position the group has taken concerning the problem, plus the rationale behind the decision in having chosen this topic.
- The students will have demonstrated the use of appropriate language in speaking to the class and in production of the final project to be turned in to the teacher and Library Media Specialist for evaluation.

Social Responsibility

CHAPTER 7

Developing Citizens for a Democratic Society

By Alice Yucht

STANDARD 7: The student who contributes positively to the learning community and to society is information literate and recognizes the importance of information to a democratic society.

Standard 7 builds on all the previous standards by recognizing that the socially responsible student is already skilled at accessing and evaluating information from a wide variety of sources, can appreciate and understand a variety of formats, and recognizes the value of increasing and sharing knowledge gained for both personal and educational purposes. A basic goal of the school library media program is to provide for students resources and activities that "represent a diversity of experiences, opinions, and social and cultural perspectives and to support the concept that intellectual freedom and access to information are prerequisite to effective and responsible citizenship in a democracy" (*Information Power*, p.7). These activities can be as complex as examining commonalities and differences in Cinderella variants or Constitutional governments, or as simple as reminding students that books borrowed must be returned so that others can use them.

Standard 7 includes two indicators, both concerned with the student's use of information resources in ways that demonstrate social responsibility about the sources themselves and about access to those sources of information. Basic to exemplary proficiency levels reflects the individual student's cognitive capabilities and social awareness. I still remember the sixth grader who took the precepts of Standard 7 very much to heart. Told that he could borrow up to four books at a time from the school library as long as he returned them on time, he appeared every Monday and Thursday afternoon to check out and return four different books. After several weeks of this, since I could discern no pattern to his selections, I asked him how he chose the books he checked out. "I use a copy of the library map you gave out," he said. "I take books from different bookcases each time, and then I check off that bookcase on the map. Sometimes the book is really interesting, and I read it all the way through. Sometimes I don't like it, so I return it right away. I only allow myself to have eight books home at a time, so sometimes I don't get to read the whole book before I have to return it. But I like exploring all kinds of different books, and I know that I can always borrow one again later if I really liked it. Can't I?"

Indicator 1 states that the socially responsible student "Seeks information from diverse sources, contexts, disciplines, and cultures." At the basic level we expect students, based on appropriate instruction, to be able to identify "several appropriate sources for resolving an information problem or question." As the students becomes more proficient they use "a variety of sources covering diverse perspectives" in their search for information, while the exemplary student will understand the value of seeking additional sources that will encompass a spectrum of "contexts, disciplines, and cultures" in order to most effectively evaluate each source's usefulness.

In "The Expert Witness" by Mary Alice

Anderson, Greg Wing, Harold Christensen, and Bob Urness, students must gather and evaluate information from a wide variety of sources about a controversial current event or issue. In this activity they need to make critical assessments about the value of both fact and opinion and take a partisan stand to defend their reasoning and judgment. "Biomedical Advantages for Athletes" also calls on students to investigate and consider the ramifications of athletes who may use questionable methods to enhance their performance. As this lesson points out, when students are working with content they are interested in, they will become very engaged in the process of comparing and contrasting opinions found in different information resources.

Indicator 2 states that the socially responsible student "Respects the principle of equitable access to information." This concept reflects the cardinal principles on which school libraries operate: that the library media program provides intellectual, physical, and equitable "access to information, ideas, and resources for learning . . . founded on a commitment to the right of intellectual freedom" (*Information Power*, p.83). At the most basic level, all students should be able to explain "why it's important for all classmates to have access to information, to information sources, and to information technology." This is the crux of every orientation lesson we do: "Here are the reasons and rules for using this (and ever other) library–to provide and have available materials for your use."

At the proficient level, the socially responsible student "Uses information, information sources, and information technology efficiently so that they are available for others

> At the most basic level, all students should be able to explain why it's important for all classmates to have access to information, to information sources, and to information technology.

to use." This carries two inferences; that the student not only can access information efficiently but also can make information accessible to others.

In the "Taste of Home" activity, students gather information about foods indigenous to a variety of cultures and then re-format the information acquired into an electronic database that others can use to see worldwide patterns of food use. While this kind of activity could be done without technology (thousands of index cards come to mind), the use of a database shows students how information can be manipulated to answer a multitude of questions.

At the exemplary level, the socially responsible student becomes an activist by proposing "strategies for ensuring that classmates and others have equitable access to information, to information sources, and to information technology." Here the student is no longer just concerned with his own use of information, but also the community's need for information. Students could certainly be encouraged to reflect on this important concept as part of "The Expert Witness" experience wherein they are required to present a point of view based on the factual information they have gathered.

Standard 7 has wide-ranging ramifications. It is imperative that our students become effective and critical information consumers. It is equally important that they understand that everyone has an equal right to the information that is or can be made available, and that this information must be accessible to all for the greater good of the community. Libraries have long been considered the "poor people's university." They must continue to be the source of choice for all lifetime learners. The socially responsible student recognizes and defends the basic principle of information access for ALL citizens.

Alice H. Yucht is a teacher-librarian at Heritage Middle School in Livingston, New Jersey.

TITLE: *A Taste of Home*

AUTHOR: Alice H. Yucht, Teacher-Librarian, Heritage Middle School, Livingston, New Jersey

CURRICULUM AREA: Geography

CURRICULUM CONNECTIONS: Home Economics, Consumer Science, Health

GRADE LEVELS: 5-7

PREREQUISITES:

■ Skills in basic search strategies, use of different kinds of resources, and database formats and uses

■ Content knowledge of ecosystems of the world, physical geography indicators of each region, kinds of foods, and preparation formats

LEARNING EXPECTATIONS/OUTCOMES:

Students will develop a database of native foods around the world that is searchable by categories (any good database software will work), including:

■ Main ingredients

■ Kind of dish (appetizer, main course, dessert, etc.)

■ Form of preparation

■ Country, area, or climate of origin

■ History or custom of food use

INFORMATION LITERACY STANDARDS FOR STUDENT LEARNING:

Standard 3, Indicators 1, 2

Standard 7, Indicator 1

MATERIALS/SOURCES NEEDED:

■ Cookbooks

■ Country books with geographic descriptions and customs

■ *Culturgrams, CIA World Factbook* (print or online)

■ Brochures, pamphlets, or menus from countries of the world

STRATEGIES:

Assign each student a different country to research. After skimming basic description or customs information about the country, student should select a specific native food to report on, and complete a worksheet listing the country, food name, and categories of information needed (see above). Students must use a minimum of three resources.

- **SESSIONS 1-2:** The library media specialist introduces special resources such as *Culturgrams* and vertical file materials and reviews techniques for skimming for information needed. Students gather information and complete worksheet. The library media specialist and teacher provide additional assistance, as needed.

- **SESSIONS 3-4:** Students continue research, if necessary, and input information into database format.

- **SESSION 5:** Students sort master database in different categories, and evaluate information patterns for commonalities and differences.

EVALUATION/CRITIQUE:

Students are evaluated on:

1 Skill at finding, noting, and categorizing needed information.

2 Variety and depth of resources used.

3 Ability to use database format to sort, comprehend, and make inferences about information.

COMMENTS/TIPS/FOLLOW-UP:

Databases are useful formats for organizing and comparing many different kinds of geographic information and for helping students understand how isolated facts can be sorted and used for different purposes.

WEB RESOURCES:

Diana's Links to International Recipes
http://titan.glo.be/diana.van.den.broek/ethnic.htm

Recipe World
http://www.recipe-world.com/

SOAR: The Searchable Online Archive of Recipes
http://soar.berkeley.edu/recipes/

TITLE: *The Expert Witness*

AUTHORS: Mary Alice Anderson, Library Media Specialist; Greg Wing, Harold Christensen, and Bob Urness, Teachers; Winona (Minnesota) Middle School.

CURRICULUM AREAS: Social studies

CURRICULUM CONNECTIONS: English, Language Arts, Health, Science

GRADE LEVELS: 7-9

PREREQUISITES:

■ Basic research skills using an online catalog, magazine databases, other online databases, reference books and some Internet searches.

■ Note taking, organizational skills, and word processing familiarity

INFORMATION LITERACY STANDARDS FOR STUDENT LEARNING:

Standard 3, Indicators 1, 4
Standard 6, Indicator 2
Standard 7, Indicator 1

CONTENT STANDARD/EXPECTATIONS:

A student shall defend a position concerning a current event or issue by demonstrating understanding of the history, facts, controversy, values, beliefs, and emotions surrounding the issue by:

■ identifying specific events or situations illustrating the impact of the issue.

■ describing a range of opinions or positions on the issue.

■ selecting and defending a position based on information.

■ describing the responsibilities of citizens involved with the issues.

■ summarizing the findings in a written, oral, or role-play presentation.

MATERIALS/SOURCES NEEDED:

■ Online catalog

■ Books

■ Periodical databases such as *Newsbank Science Source, ProQuest, Middle Search, Gale Net DISCovering Science* and *DISCovering Multicultural America*

■ Note-taking forms

■ Word processing software

■ Daily newspapers, both print copy and online

STRATEGIES:

1 The teacher gives the students the topic list and spends a class period discussing possible topics and preparing students for the project. Give students handout outlining project requirements and specific requirements for oral and written presentations.

2 The library media specialist prepares a search strategy form which students will use to brainstorm ideas, record sources, and take notes.

3 When students come to the media center, the library media specialist reviews resources with the students and introduces them to any sources and strategies they may not have used extensively. (TASK I) The periodical database is stressed to emphasize the importance of periodicals for topics of this nature. Mention is made of local resources, such as the community web site that will be of interest to students studying local issues.

4 The research process takes approximately seven to eight days. Students alternate time in the media center with time in the classroom. Classroom time is spent organizing the information and meeting with the teacher about their progress. During second and third visits to the media center, the library media specialist provides instruction on resources that have emerged as being especially useful. The library media specialist works individually with students who are having problems. Note-taking and bibliographic skills are stressed. Do not allow students to print articles from electronic resources.

5 Students spend two to three class periods organizing their information.

6 Students spend two to three class periods word processing the information.

7 Two to three class periods are usually necessary for oral presentations.

EVALUATION/CRITIQUE:

All phases of the project are assessed. Students are assessed on both the process and the product.

Task management skills
Resource Management:
- access information efficiently and effectively
- proper use and care of materials, equipment, and facilities
- share materials appropriately

Perseverance:
- focus on the task for appropriate length of time
- continue to try despite frustrations, distractions, and obstacles
- attend to details and check for errors

STUDENT HANDOUT

OVERVIEW:

In this performance package, you will examine a current event or issue, take a position on the issue, and defend that position. In order to complete the package, you will need to prepare and present an oral testimony or a written summary of the current event or issue chosen. To begin:

- Select a topic. Research a current event or issue and select a topic for further study. Your teacher must approve your topic before you proceed.
- Gather information. Using resources available to you, gather information on your topic. You will use this information to prepare either an oral presentation or a written summary.

ABOUT YOUR SOURCES:

1 You must use at least three sources of information.

2 Your sources must be varied and present facts and opinions that represent a range of viewpoints on the issue, for example, Internet, books, magazines, newspapers, and interviews of adults. If your issue is featured in a video, or on a television or radio report, a broader range of perspectives might be presented. Therefore be sure you have enough different kinds of sources to provide facts from various perspectives and a range of opinions.

3 Identify the role of the author, or the subject of each story, report, or interview. As you are learning about the issue, think about which perspectives you understand and would best represent in your oral presentation or your written summary. When you present your oral presentation or your written summary, you will be taking a particular viewpoint and defending that position. You will be questioned regarding the sources.

4 Cite your sources carefully.

ABOUT RECORDING YOUR NOTES:

1 Take detailed notes.

2 Use index cards for reference notes as you make your oral presentation.

3 You will need to transfer the information from your notes to a more formal format for your written summary. Directions for that format are attached.

4 Arrange to have your teacher check your progress at appropriate times. Your teacher will help you determine if you have a sufficient variety of sources.

ABOUT PREPARING YOUR PRESENTATION:

After you have gathered and recorded your information about the current event or issue, take a position and prepare to defend it. Develop an outline and have it approved by your teacher. The following is necessary for either an oral presentation or a written summary.

1 Oral presentation presents your point of view and a summary of the history, controversy, and your defense of your position. This presentation should be approximately four minutes long. Prepare your speech in the following format:

- **INTRODUCTION:** Prepare a thesis statement clearly defining your position.

- **BACKGROUND:** Give a historical background of your topic using the historical information you have gathered.

- **VIEWPOINTS:** Give a brief summary of the points of view that currently exist in regard to this issue. Explain why disagreement exists.

- **YOUR POSITION:** Define the issue in a way that makes your position clear. Be sure to give support to each of your major points. Include examples of situations to illustrate how the issue is making or has made impact on people's lives. Specific information about actual people, events, or situations will strengthen your viewpoint. Show how recognized experts or current studies support your position. Describe how citizens involved with the issues have taken on certain responsibilities.

- **CONCLUSION:** Prepare a concluding statement and be ready to answer questions you may receive from your teacher or classmates. You will probably be asked questions such as:

  Where did you get your information?

  How recent is your information?

  How many people were affected or are still being affected by this issue?

  How many other people hold this same position as yours?

  What are other viewpoints on the subject?

- **TIP:** Practice your presentation several times. Use your notes to help you as you are speaking.

2 Write your summary, presenting information that includes your point of view and a summary of the history, controversy, and defense of your position. Use your notes and outline to develop a written document of a minimum of three pages (word processed, doubled-spaced, 12-point font size (Bookman, Chicago, Times, Geneva, or Helvetica) with one-inch margins (title page, and source list not included in the number of pages required). You will give this document to your teacher. Your written report should be prepared in the following way:

- **TITLE PAGE:** Include the issue, your name, and the current date.

- **INTRODUCTION:** Prepare a thesis statement clearly defining your position.

- **BACKGROUND:** Give a historical background of your topic using historical information you have gathered.

- **VIEWPOINTS:** Give a brief summary of the existing points of view in regard to this issue. Most of your paper should explain your own position. Discuss the controversy surrounding your current event or issue. Explain why disagreement exists.

- **YOUR POSITION:** Define the issue in a way that makes your position clear. Be sure to give support to each of your major points. Include examples of situations to illustrate how the issue is making or has made impact on people's lives; specific information about actual people, events, or situations; show how recognized experts or current studies support your position; describe the responsibilities of citizens involved with the issues.

■ **CONCLUSION:** Prepare a concluding statement and be ready to answer questions from your teacher or Library Media Specialist.

■ **BIBLIOGRAPHY:** List the sources that you used for this project (see format sheet).

■ Spell-check and proofread your written product. Attend to all details and correct any errors.

ORAL PRESENTATION FEEDBACK CHECKLIST:

The purpose of this checklist is to provide feedback to the student about his or her work relative to the content standard. Have the standard available for reference. Both student and teacher (or Library Media Specialist) complete checklist.

Y = Yes
N = Needs Improvement

ORAL PRESENTATION

TEACHER		STUDENT
_____	Thesis statement clearly defines position.	_____
_____	Historical background of topic is given.	_____
_____	Summarizes different existing points of view.	_____
_____	Explains the controversy surrounding topic.	_____
_____	Stated position is well-defined.	_____
_____	Each major point is supported with examples.	_____
_____	Shows how recognized experts and/or current studies support position.	_____
_____	Describes responsibilities of citizens involved with the issue.	_____
_____	Has a concluding statement.	_____
_____	Uses at least three sources.	_____
_____	Is approximately four minutes in length.	_____
_____	Outline is prepared and if using note cards, they are prepared.	_____

WRITTEN PRESENTATION FEEDBACK CHECKLIST:

The purpose of this checklist is to provide feedback to the student about his or her work relative to the content standard. Have the standard available for reference. Student and teachers (or library media specialist) complete checklist.

Y = Yes
N = Needs Improvement

Student	WRITTEN PRESENTATION	Teacher
_____	Thesis statement clearly defines position.	_____
_____	Historical background of topic is given.	_____
_____	Summarizes different existing points of view.	_____
_____	Explains the controversy surrounding topic.	_____
_____	Stated position is well-defined.	_____
_____	Each major point is supported with examples.	_____
_____	Shows how recognized experts and/or current studies support position.	_____
_____	Describes responsibilities of citizens involved with the issue.	_____
_____	Has a concluding statement.	_____
_____	Uses at least three sources.	_____
_____	Outline is prepared.	_____
_____	Information is presented in proper format:	_____
_____	■ minimum of three pages	_____
_____	■ doubled spaced	_____
_____	■ number 12 font size in Bookman, Chicago, Times, Geneva, Helvetica	_____
_____	■ one-inch margins	_____
_____	Bibliography done in proper format.	_____

COMMENTS/TIPS/FOLLOW-UP:

1 This unit is called a *performance package*, the term for large instructional units used to assess achievement on the Minnesota graduation standards. The media specialist and teachers spent over ten hours collaboratively planning this package. This involved identifying topics, selecting the best resources, and designing search forms for the students. A half day was used to review the project after the first group of students had implemented it. This time was also used to plan for future resource acquisitions, review instructional strategies and update the topic list.

2 Our students complete the Expert Witness unit in seventh grade, but it is probably more developmentally appropriate for eighth or ninth grade. It should not be implemented with seventh grade students in the fall unless they have had previous experience with this type of research project.

3 The Internet is not the best resource for this project when used with younger students. Too many materials are not developmentally appropriate and there is far too much information for the students to use efficiently. For some topics, especially those about local and state issues, the Internet can be useful, but for most, we found books provided basic background information and a variety of opinions.

4 State graduation standards and performance packages are highly dependent on non-textbook resources and the information literacy process. The expectations placed on teachers to help students prepare the packages have led to more intensive use of media center resources as well as careful and thorough instructional design. As a state graduation standard performance package it does strongly address Information Literacy Standard 6, pursuing excellence in the information process. It is very difficult for a student to achieve a high score on this project.

STUDENT HANDOUT

NOTE-TAKING FORM SAMPLE:

Subtopic:_____   Card Number:_____

Topic:_____   Student Name:_____

_____

_____

_____

_____

_____

TOPIC LIST:

Abortion	Internet filtering
Academic pressure	Juvenile detention centers
Addiction	Landfills
Aggression	Lyric censorship
AIDS	Obsessive compulsive disorder
Alzheimer's disease	Peer pressure
Animal rights	Pesticides
Anorexia nervosa	Post traumatic stress disorder
At-risk children	Private rights of public people
Athletic pressure	Rape
Body image	Recycling
Bulimia	Runaways
Capital punishment	School dress code
Censorship	School uniforms
Chewing tobacco	Self esteem
Cloning	Sexual abuse
Community notification laws	Single parents
Death	Steroids
Depression	Stress
DNA testing as evidence	Suicide
Doctor-assisted suicide	Sun over-exposure
Ebonics	Teen curfew
Family abuse	Teenage parenting
Gambling	Teenage pregnancy
Garbage	Teenage violence
Gun Control	Teens in prison
Guns in school	Trying juveniles as adults
Hazardous waste	Weight control
Home schools	Welfare reform
Homeless children	Working students
Illegal drugs	Year-round school
Immigration	

ALIGNMENT OF FEEDBACK CHECKLIST WITH STANDARD AND TASK DESCRIPTION

The purpose of this alignment is to be sure that there is an item for each part of the standard being assessed and to be sure that everything being assessed has been asked for in the task description.

ORAL PRESENTATION

Standard   **Task Description**

_____   Thesis statement clearly defines position.

_____   Historical background of topic is given.

_____   Summarizes different existing points of view.

_____   Explains the controversy surrounding topic.

_____   Stated position is well-defined.

_____   Each major point is supported with examples.

_____   Shows how recognized experts and / or current studies support position.

_____   Describes responsibilities of citizens involved with the issue.

_____   Has a concluding statement.

_____   Uses at least three sources.

_____   Is approximately four minutes in length.

_____   Outline is prepared. If using notecards, they are prepared.

ALIGNMENT OF FEEDBACK CHECKLIST WITH STANDARD AND TASK DESCRIPTION

The purpose of this alignment is to be sure that there is an item for each part of the standard being assessed and to be sure that everything being assessed has been asked for in the task description.

WRITTEN PRESENTATION

Standard   **Task Description**

_____   Thesis statement clearly defines position.

_____   Historical background of topic is given.

_____   Summarizes different existing points of view.

_____   Explains the controversy surrounding your topic.

_____   Stated position is well-defined.

_____   Each major point is supported with examples.

_____   Shows how recognized experts and / or current studies support position.

_____   Describes responsibilities of citizens involved with the issue.

_____   Has a concluding statement.

_____   Uses at least three resources

_____   Outline is prepared.

_____   Information is presented in proper format:

■ minimum of three pages

■ doubled spaced

■ number 12 font size in Bookman, Chicago, Times, Geneva, or Helvetica

■ one inch margins

_____   Bibliography done in proper format

SKILLS:

TASK 1: Prepare a written, oral, or role-play presentation on a current issue.

Know		Teach
_____	Using automated catalog	_____
_____	Using search strategies	_____
_____	Taking notes	_____
_____	Preparing an outline	_____
_____	Developing a thesis statement	_____
_____	Selecting appropriate materials	_____
_____	Making a bibliography	_____
_____	Recording sources	_____
_____	Determining what information is relevant	_____
_____	Defending a position with relevant proof	_____
_____	Evaluating information	_____
_____	Browsing for idea	_____
_____	Identifying a variety of potential sources of information	_____
_____	Selecting information appropriate to the issue	_____
_____	Sharing knowledge and information with others	_____
_____	Producing and communicating information and ideas in appropriate formats	_____

TITLE: *Biomedical Advantages for Athletes*

AUTHOR: Alice H. Yucht, Teacher-Librarian, Heritage Middle School, Livingston, New Jersey

CURRICULUM AREA: Health

CURRICULUM CONNECTIONS: Biology, Ethics

GRADE LEVEL: 11-12

PREREQUISITES:

■ Research skills in use of periodical databases, online search strategies, and familiarity with discriminating between fact and opinion

■ Content knowledge of human physiology, anatomy, and sports training

INFORMATION LITERACY STANDARDS FOR STUDENT LEARNING:

Standard 2, Indicators 1-4
Standard 4, Indicators 1, 2
Standard 7, Indicator 1

INTRODUCTION:

Students will investigate and report on current techniques, strategies, and controversies concerning improving athletic performance in Olympic sports events.

MATERIALS/SOURCES NEEDED:

Wide variety of current periodicals, reports, and Web sites, as identified through databases such as *Reader's Guide, InfoTrak, ProQuest,* and *Electric Library,* and use of search engines such as *Yahoo, Dogpile,* and *Beaucoup.*

STRATEGIES:

■ Students each choose a sport, and identify benchmarks of excellence in that sport.

■ Students must locate, read, and summarize a minimum of five different articles on their topic.

STEPS:

1 Library Media Specialist will instruct or review search strategies for using specific databases available.

2 Library Media Specialist will instruct or review use of different kinds of online search engines.

3 Library Media Specialist will review appropriate citation formats for articles and Web sites.

4 Library Media Specialist will review strategies for evaluating information sources for accuracy and bias.

EVALUATION/CRITIQUE:

Students will be evaluated on:

■ variety of resources used.

■ summaries of information gathered.

■ explanation of accuracy, relevance, and possible applications of information gathered.

COMMENTS/TIPS/FOLLOW-UP:

This kind of "targeted" high-interest information search is very useful for getting students to compare and contrast information from a variety of current sources, and understand the need to evaluate the accuracy and authority of their sources

CHAPTER 8

Developing Ethical Behaviors

By Tami J. Little

STANDARD 8: The student who contributes positively to the learning community and to society is information literate and practices ethical behavior in regard to information and information technology.

According to *Information Power: Building Partnerships for Learning*, a student who meets this standard "applies principles and practices that reflect high ethical standards for accessing, evaluating, and using information." The student also "recognizes the importance of equitable access to information in a democratic society and respects the principles of intellectual freedom and the rights of producers of intellectual property" (*Information Power*, p. 36).

When looking more closely at this standard, it is evident that social responsibility is often overlooked in traditional lessons. It is the responsibility of teachers and library media specialists to design lessons requiring students to use higher-order thinking skills and meet high standards for ethical behavior. Provided the teacher and library media specialist have designed the lesson using an information-processing framework, students will have an understanding of concepts related to intellectual property and the importance of proper citation of sources.

There are three indicators for Standard 8, each of which includes three levels of proficiency: basic, proficient, and exemplary. Indicator 1 states that the student who meets this standard "respects the principles of intellectual freedom." At the basic level, the student is able to define or give examples of "intellectual freedom." At the proficient level, the student "analyzes a situation in terms of its relationship to intellectual freedom." At the exemplary level, the student "predicts what might happen if the principles of intellectual freedom were ignored in one's own community."

Students can encourage others to exercise their rights to free expression, respect the ideas of others when working in groups, and actively solicit ideas from every member of the group. Students are introduced to this concept by working in cooperative groups. Students in groups learn that each group member has a role and that everyone's ideas are important. Multicultural education also plays an important role in this indicator. Children who are able to respect the ideas of those from other cultures will have more success meeting this indicator.

Indicator 2 states that the student respects intellectual property rights. At the basic level, the student "gives examples of what it means to respect intellectual property rights." At the proficient level the student "analyzes situations to determine the steps necessary to respect intellectual property rights." At the exemplary level the student "avoids plagiarism, cites sources properly, makes copies and incorporates text and images only with appropriate clearance, etc., when creating information products."

When students understand the concept of fair use and apply it, they recognize and diligently avoid plagiarism. Students who follow an information-seeking process to come to their own conclusions express ideas in their own words rather than copying the conclusions or arguments presented by others, and they follow bibliographic form and cite all information sources used. Fair use and intellectual property are complex concepts and the importance of helping middle and secondary school students learn ethical behaviors is emphasized in several of the lessons in this chapter.

The "Career Pathfinder" is an excellent example of how the teacher and librarian can teach students to record information without plagiarizing, while "Battle of the University Artists: Who Gets the Job?" expects students to respect intellectual property rights by teaching them to cite all sources. "Cyberspace Planet Exploration" uses a note taking sheet to help the students record information in their own words.

In order for students to be able to clearly perform Indicator 2, the teacher and library media specialist must design lessons accordingly. Lessons requiring the regurgitation of facts enable students to plagiarize. If the lesson is written in such a way that the students follow an information-seeking process to demonstrate learning, then Indicator 2 becomes easier to achieve. Students can use the information they find to produce a product demonstrating their knowledge. Many of the lessons included throughout this book apply this principle. In "Cyberspace Planet Exploration" Deb Logan actually tells students at the beginning of the activity they will need to go beyond merely restating the facts. Joyce Valenza's "Battle of the University Artists: Who Gets the Job?" requires students to produce a multimedia resumé. The task assessment list included with her lesson requires students and teachers to consider a wide variety of criteria as the product is evaluated.

> Students who follow an information seeking process to come to their own conclusions express ideas in their own words rather than copying the conclusions or arguments presented by others...

One skill that both teachers and librarians should teach is note taking. Methods of note taking include QUAD, KWL, check sheets, pathfinders, graphic organizers, and fact sheets. "Career Pathfinder" by Deb Logan includes model note-taking sheets and a topic organizer web that library media specialists can use to guide seventh and eighth grade students in mastering this skill.

Indicator 3 states that students use information technology responsibly. At the basic level of proficiency, the student "states the main points of school policy on using computing and communications hardware, software, and networks." At the proficient level, the student "locates appropriate information efficiently with the school's computing and communications hardware, software, and networks." At the exemplary level, the student "follows all school guidelines related to the use of computing and communications hardware, software, and networks when resolving information problems or questions."

Students must be taught to follow acceptable use policies and guidelines, use equipment for the purposes intended, and leave the equipment and materials in good working order. Doug Johnson (article available online at **http://www.infotoday.com/**

MMSchools/nov98/johnson.htm) describes how students can identify right from wrong using the "3Ps of Technology Ethics":

JOHNSON'S 3 P'S OF TECHNOLOGY ETHICS:

1 PRIVACY—I will protect my privacy and respect the privacy of others.

2 PROPERTY—I will protect my property and respect the property of others.

3 APPROPRIATE USE—I will use technology in constructive ways and in ways which do not break the rules of my family, church, school, or government.

A student who meets Standard 8 "applies principles and practices that reflect high ethical standards for accessing, evaluating, and using information." The student also "recognizes the importance of equitable access to information in a democratic society and respects the principles of intellectual freedom and the rights of producers of intellectual property" (*Information Power*, p. 36).

Tamara J. Little is a Librarian at Hinton (Iowa) Community School.

TITLE: *Cyberspace Planet Exploration*

AUTHOR: Debra Kay Logan, Librarian/Media Specialist, Taft Middle School, Marion, Ohio

CURRICULUM AREA: Science

CURRICULUM CONNECTIONS: Language Arts, Fine Arts

GRADE LEVELS: 7-8

PREREQUISITES: Topic skills, Dewey and electronic search strategies

INFORMATION LITERACY STANDARDS FOR STUDENT LEARNING:
Standard 2, Indicators 1, 3, 4
Standard 3, Indicators 1, 4
Standard 8, Indicators 2, 3

MATERIALS/SOURCES NEEDED:

- Cyberspace Planet Exploration note-taking sheets and storyboarding sheets
- Chalk or dry erase board
- Computer, scanner, blank disks, CD-ROM resources, Internet access
- Multimedia projector or LCD panel
- Books, magazines
- Presentation program such as Hyperstudio or PowerPoint

STRATEGIES:

1 Working in groups of two (three if computer access mandates), students will research a planet, then plan and create a multimedia presentation about that planet.

2 Students will collect pictures of the planets from the Internet or scan print pictures and save to disks for use in multimedia presentations. All sources should be cited.

STEPS:

1 Introduce this unit by showing past projects or sample Hyperstudio and PowerPoint presentations. Explain to students they will be creating their own presentations.

2 Present the note-taking sheet as a starting point. Review the sheet with students, clarifying any unfamiliar vocabulary or concepts. Encourage students to collect information beyond the note-taking sheet. Be prepared to explain elliptical orbits. A quick diagram on the chalk or dry erase board is very effective.

3 Initially, students will probably think of this as a "know the facts and give the right answers" type of project. When discussing and planning where to search for information, encourage students to think about how what we "know" about the planets is constantly changing. Then ask them to identify optimal research sources. (Almanacs, recent encyclopedias, new books, new CD-ROMs, and current online resources.)

4 A large part of gathering information for this project will be to collect graphics of a planet. Using the multimedia projector or LCD panel, demonstrate saving images to disk. If a projection system is not available, guide students through the steps as they sit at workstations. Emphasize ethical use of information resources at this time. Have students record the sources of all images used. Make it clear that sources need to be cited when any image is used. Post on a chalk or white board the information needed to credit the sources:

a. name of Web site

b. author of Web site (if available)

c. most recent date of Web site

d. address of Web site

5 Hyperstudio may crash if numerous large graphic files are imported. Therefore limit the number of imported graphics to three or four. Also beware of large files (with many graphics) that cannot be saved to the standard 3.5 inch disk.

6 After gathering information and images, students will need to know what the presentation software can do and how to use it. Even if the students are already familiar with presentation software, remind them of the available options. After trying detailed step-by-step sheets, I have had the most success by using the multimedia projector to walk students through these program features:

a. creating a new card/slide set

b. celecting or creating a background

c. inserting and formatting text

d. inserting graphics, sounds, tables, etc.

e. navigating within the program

f. saving the work.

After the walk through, let students experiment for at least half of a period.

7 Once familiar with the software, students need to plan how they want to present their facts using the presentation program. It may take an entire class period to explain the concept of storyboarding before students can storyboard their projects. Point out they will need to group and sequence their information and use of graphics. They will also need to determine how many cards/slides they will be creating.

8 Assist students as they are working. While the research phase of this project is fairly simple, the copying of images, storyboarding and creation of presentations may be totally new experiences. **Remind students to save their work frequently.**

WRAP-UP:

Using a multimedia projector, have students share their projects with the whole class.

EVALUATION:
Use Cyberspace Planet Project Check Sheet.

Name: _____

CYBERSPACE PLANET PROJECT CHECK SHEET

	NOT YET! 😦	SOMETIMES 😐	OFTEN 🙂	YES! 😃
Project is full of information, all of which is accurate, clear, complete and detailed.				
Sources are credited.				
Writing is neat, easy to read, and makes sense.				
Punctuation, spelling, and grammar are correct.				
Work is labeled in a way that explains the project. Labels are clear and full of details.				
Followed directions and used time well.				
Project was well planned: neat, original and easy to use.				
Presentation was loud and easy to hear. Visual aids were well used.				

COMMENTS/TIPS/FOLLOW UP:

■ This activity will require seven to ten class periods. Gathering information and graphics will take approximately two of the periods. The overall timing depends on the availability of computers with presentation program software, such Hyperstudio or PowerPoint. Additional independent research and project time may be needed.

■ Adjust this unit to limited computers or software by having students create a group presentation project. Students as a group determine the basic facts to be included for each planet. Have one or two sets of partners come to the library/media center from class to work on their card/slides in the stack. Remaining information can be part of a written report, oral presentation, or other product.

■ The group stack approach described above can be used with special needs students as well. Plan to work with each team as they develop their card/slides. Further modify the unit by creating a planet fact writing template with students.

■ Using Hyperstudio or a similar program, create a Cyberspace Planet Jeopardy game. Each team can create a game for their planet or the game could be a group stack effort as described above. Images are used as visual clues.

Name:_____

CYBERSPACE PLANET FACT SHEET

My planet is _____. It is the _____ planet from the sun.
              (planet's name)   (position number)

PLANET FACTS:

1 Diameter (how far across): _____ miles

2 Distance from the sun: greatest: _____miles   least: _____miles

3 Distance from the earth: greatest: _____miles   least: _____miles

4 Length of year (how long it takes to orbit the sun): _____ earth days & hours

5 Length of day (how long it takes to rotate): _____ earth days & hours

6 Temperature: high _____ low _____degrees Fahrenheit/Celsius (circle one)

7 Draw the sign for the planet in the empty box.

8 Does this planet have satellites? _____How many? _____What are their names?

_____

9 Describe the make-up of the planet's atmosphere._____

10 What is the planet's weather like?_____

11 What do we know about the planet's surface?_____

_____

12 Share any special features or interesting facts about this planet.

_____

_____

STORYBOARDING SHEET:

Team: _____

STORYBOARD SHEET

_____

_____

_____

_____

_____

_____

_____

_____

_____

_____

_____

_____

_____

_____

_____

_____

TITLE: *Career Pathfinder*

AUTHOR: Debra Kay Logan, Librarian/Media Specialist, Taft Middle School, Marion, Ohio.

CURRICULUM AREA: Life Skills

CURRICULUM CONNECTIONS: Language Arts, Information Skills

GRADE LEVEL: 8

PREREQUISITES: topic skills, Dewey and electronic search strategies

INFORMATION LITERACY STANDARDS FOR STUDENT LEARNING:
Standard 1, Indicators 1, 2, 4, 5
Standard 2, Indicators 1-4
Standard 8, Indicators 1, 3

MATERIALS/SOURCES NEEDED:
Career Pathfinder Sheet
Career Topic Organizer
Web Check sheet
Research Sources sheets
Career Pathfinder Mini Check Sheet
Career Exploration Notes (optional)
Computer workstations
Subject area books and magazines
CD-ROM resources and Internet access

STRATEGIES:
- Ask students if they usually start taking notes as soon as they find information. (Every hand will probably go up.)
- Then ask if they ever wonder if the source is worthwhile or if there might be better information elsewhere.
- Introduce or reinforce the concept of evaluating information by telling students they will be looking for the best possible resources and creating a pathfinder to information on the career of his or her choice. I like to ask them if they are sitting down and then tell them that they will NOT be taking notes!
- Emphasize their job will be to design a career pathfinder that will enable the user to find selected and recommended information on a particular career. By having to find as many resources as possible to evaluate, they may be surprised to find how much information is available, both reliable and unreliable.

STEPS:

1 Distribute the Career Pathfinder sheet. Tell students this will be part of their final product and they should not start completing it until they have located and evaluated their resources.

2 Use the Career Pathfinder sheet as a guide to discuss possible resources and their availability in the library/media center.

3 Review basic search strategies like Boolean logic and the use of any type of index. Remind students the Dewey system groups materials by topic so it is a good idea to check neighboring materials on the shelf.

4 Using the Career Topic Organizer, review the topic skills. Ask students, With the topic of your career, how could you:

- broaden the topic?
- narrow the topic?
- restate the topic?
- find related topics?

Have students use their Career Topic Organizers to brainstorm possible search terms.

5 Have students look at their Web Check sheet. I tell my students I have some good news for them: they do not need to evaluate any of the resources in the library/media center, because they were all evaluated when they were purchased and they all are checked for currency at least once every three years. But Internet sites do need to be evaluated. Discuss the things students need to look for when evaluating Web sites and ask them to predict where on a Web site this type of information is likely to be found.

- **Author**: Is the site signed? Would you buy a book if the author did not sign their name? Is there a way to contact the author?

- **Authority**: Is he or she qualified to write the site? Is there evidence that he or she did the research?

- **Currency**: When was the site created? When was the site updated? Can you tell?

- **Source**: What type of domain does the site have? (See below.)

  .com stands for commercial and **.net** stands for Internet. Commercial sites can have an agenda that may or may not influence the quality of information on sites. Sometimes the information is excellent. These Web sites may be excellent resources, but they may also be unreliable. Look for clues as to the reliability of .com or .net sites.

  .ac is a domain for university or college. **.edu** stands for school or university. **.k12** is a public school domain. Education web sites can be excellent information sites, but they can be inaccurate as well. Is the site the work of a student or teacher? Which do you think is more likely to be accurate? Was the site done for an assignment or for fun? Look at who is responsible for the site and why it was written.

  .gov stands for government and **.mil** stands for military. Depending on the government responsible for the site, these are usually considered to be very reliable Web sites. Among the United States .gov sites are NASA, Library of Congress and the Smithsonian Museum.

.org is the domain for organizations. Some organizations are research-based and seek to share the most current and accurate information. Other organizations are biased and exist to manipulate the way that people think. Think about the type of organization and thus their purpose for having the site. Give students examples of organizations like the Red Cross, the American Diabetes Association, a neo-Nazi group, and ask your students to predict the type of message likely to be found on each of these Web sites.

What is your **overall** opinion of the Web site? Does the information appear to be fact or opinion? Does the site have typographical mistakes, grammatical errors or other obvious "sloppy" editing problems? Is the site easy to use?

6 Discuss the Research Sources sheets and how to complete the sheets for different types of resources.

7 Share and discuss Career Pathfinder Check Sheet.

8 Assist students as they search for potential resources.

9 Remind them their goal is to create a path that anyone can follow to learn about their career of choice.

WRAP UP:

10 On the final research day, remind students to fill out their Career Pathfinder sheet. Ask them to think about which search words worked the best and what strategies would they recommend to any searcher?

11 Ask students if they were surprised by the amount of information to be found on a single topic. Another good question to ask is, "In the past when you have used the first available information, did you miss other great information?"

EVALUATION:
Use the Career Pathfinder Mini Check Sheet to evaluate students' work.

Name: _____

CAREER PATHFINDER MINI CHECK SHEET

	NOT YET! ☹	SOMETIMES 😐	OFTEN 🙂	YES! 😀
Used a variety of information tools.				
Evaluated resources. Made sure source is reliable by checking author, authority, currency, and source.				
Filled out appropriate sections of the Research Sources form.				
Created a clear path to reliable information.				
Used time well.				

Comments on the back.

COMMENTS/TIPS/FOLLOW-UP:

1 Allow at least five research periods for this project. I do this project in collaboration with our language arts teachers. Since they have double periods, I introduce the lesson to the whole class and then divide students into two groups. We then alternate the two groups, which allows students better access to limited resources.

2 Always remind students they are expected to have all their work materials with them when they report to the library/media center.

3 When the assignment is finished, invite students to follow their own Career Pathfinder sheets. A Career Exploration notes sheet is available to students who wish to follow Career Pathfinder sheets and explore their own career choices.

Name:_____

CAREER PATHFINDER

1 **CAREER**: _____

2 **POSSIBLE SEARCH TERMS**:

    a. _____

    b. _____

    c. _____

    d. _____

    e. _____

3 **SOURCES** where information about this career is to be found.

    e. encyclopedias ☐

    e. Internet ☐

    e. almanac ☐

    e. specialized reference book ☐

    e. books via the card catalog ☐

    e. magazine ☐

    e. expert ☐

    e. other _____ ☐

4 For each source in which information is found there should be an entry on the **RESEARCH SOURCES SHEETS**.

5 **COMMENTS AND SUGGESTIONS** for searchers: _____

_____

_____

_____

CAREER TOPIC ORGANIZER

Name:_____

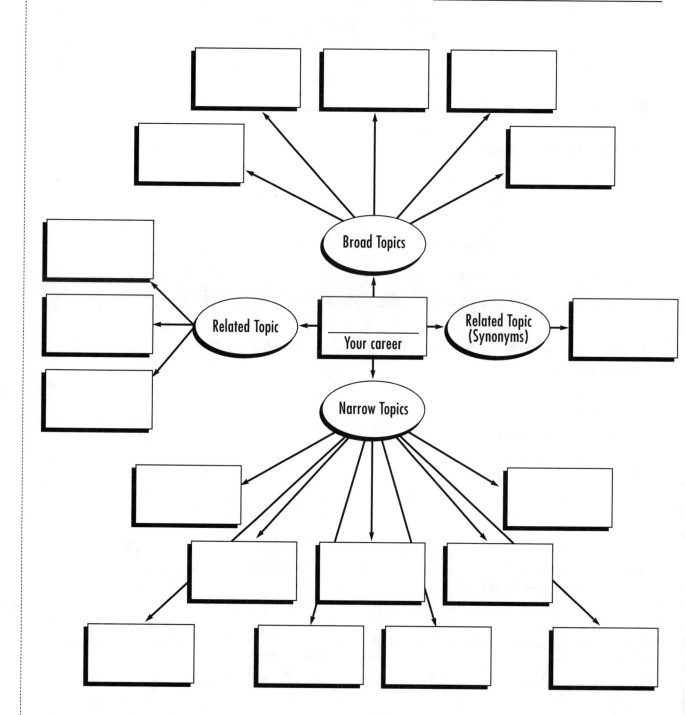

WEB CHECK SHEET

Name:_____

DIRECTIONS:
Using check +, check and
check –, rate the web sites
you find.

WEB SITE NAME	AUTHOR Is it signed? Is there a way to contact the author?	AUTHOR Is it signed? Is there a way to contact the author?	CURRENCY When was the site created & last updated? Is this information easy to locate?	SOURCE What is the site's domain? Is it .com, .net, .gov, .mil, .k12, .ac, .edu, or .org?	OVERALL Does the site have facts, opinions, mistakes or good info? Is it easy to use?	RATING Great! OK… No!

RESOURCE SOURCES

Name: _____

RESOURCE	TITLE	AUTHOR	DATE	PUBLISHER	PLACE OF PUBLICATION	URL (Internet address)	RATING
Books	x	x	x	x	x		
Encyclopedias	x and volume #	x (if given)	x	x	x		
Expert	name	x	of interview		place of interview		
Magazines	x article & magazine	x	x				
Internet Sites	x	x (if given)	searched & of info			x	
CD-ROM's	x	x (if given)	x	x	x		

RESOURCE	TITLE	AUTHOR	DATE	PUBLISHER	PLACE OF PUBLICATION	URL (Internet address)	RATING

RESOURCE SOURCES

Name: _____

RESOURCE	TITLE	AUTHOR	DATE	PUBLISHER	PLACE OF PUBLICATION	URL (Internet address)	RATING

CAREER EXPLORATION SHEET:

Name:_____

CAREER EXPLORATION NOTES

Career: _____

Salary range: _____

Job outlook: _____

Brief description of career: _____

_____

_____

Skills needed for this job: _____

_____

_____

Types of responsibilities: _____

_____

_____

Training for career:

Years: _____ Education: _____

Schools offering training for this field:

1 _____

2 _____

TITLE: *Battle of the University Artists: Who Gets the Job?*

AUTHOR: Joyce Kasman Valenza, Librarian, Springfield Township (Pennsylvania) High School

CURRICULUM AREA: Art, History

CURRICULUM CONNECTIONS: Language Arts, Information Skills

INFORMATION LITERACY STANDARDS FOR STUDENT LEARNING:
Standard 5, Indicator 3
Standard 7, Indicator 1
Standard 8, Indicator 2

GRADE LEVELS: 9-12

PREREQUISITES: A basic knowledge of multimedia authoring software and basic experience with Internet searching

LEARNING EXPECTATIONS/OUTCOMES:
- Students will deepen their knowledge of a famous artist.
- Students will gain practice searching for biographical information and learn about the art resources of the Web.
- Students will learn to prepare an effective resume and cover letter.
- Students will gain experience in persuasive communication using multimedia.

MATERIALS/SOURCES NEEDED:
- Web browser for research
- Hyperstudio, PowerPoint or other multimedia authoring software
- Word processing software for resume
- Other print and video materials
- Style sheet for bibliographic citation
- Presentation equipment for student projects

WEB RESOURCES:

1 Students should try browsing through art books or museum Web sites if they need help selecting an artist whose work they admire. Once they find an artist, the best approach may be using a subject directory such as the Britannica Internet Guide (**http://www.britannica.com/**).

2 There are also a variety of art gateway sites worth bookmarking, distributing in handout form, or gathering on a Web page prior to beginning this project.

Gateway sites for art include:

Art History Research Centre	http://www-fofa.concordia.ca/arth/AHRC/index.htm
Art History Resources on the Web	http://witcombe.sbc.edu/ARTHLinks.html
ARTSEDGE	http://artsedge.kennedy-center.org/artsedge.html
Gateway to Art History	http://www.harbrace.com/art/gardner/
Artcyclopedia	http://artcyclopedia.com/
ArtsEdNet	http://www.artsednet.getty.edu/
ArtServe: Australian National University	http://rubens.anu.edu.au/index2.html
Cyburbia	http://www.arch.buffalo.edu/pairc
History of Art Textbook	http://www.prenhallart.com/html/learn/book1.htm
Incredible Art Department	http://www.artswire.org/kenroar
Modern Masterworks	http://hyperion.advanced.org/17142/home.shtml
WebMuseum Artists Index	http://metalab.unc.edu/wm/paint/auth/
Yahoo Arts Masters	http://dir.yahoo.com/Arts/Artists/Masters/
Yahoo Art History: Periods & Movements	http://dir.yahoo.com/Arts/Art_History/Periods_and_Movements/

Museums Sites include:

American Museum of Photography	http://www.photographymuseum.com/
Art Museum Network	http://www.amn.org/
Asian Arts	http://www.webart.com/asianart/index.html
Brooklyn Museum, New York	http://www.brooklynart.org/
Dallas Museum of Art	http://www.dm-art.org/
Delaware Art Museum	http://www.delart.mus.de.us
Detroit Institute of the Arts	http://www.dia.org
Louvre	http://www.paris.org/Musees/Louvre/
Metropolitan Museum of Art	http://www.metmuseum.org/htmlfile/education/edu.html
Minneapolis Institute of Arts	http://www.artsmia.org/
Musee	http://www.musee-online.org
Museum Index at World Wide Arts Resources	http://wwar.com/museums.html
Galleria degli Uffizi	http://www.televisual.it/uffizi/
George Eastman House Museum	http://www.eastman.org/
Guggenheim Museum	http://www.guggenheim.org/
Museum of Modern Art, New York	http://www.moma.org/docs/menu/index.htm

National Museum of American Art	**http://nmaa-ryder.si.edu/**
National Museum of Women in the Arts	**http://www.nmwa.org/index.htm**
Philadelphia Museum of Art	**http://pma.libertynet.org**
Salvadore Dali Museum	**http://www.webcoast.com/Dali/**
Smart Museum of Art	**http://smartmuseum.uchicago.edu**
Smithsonian Institution	**http://www.si.edu**
Smithsonian Photographs Online	**http://photo2.si.edu/index.html**
The Thinker Fine Art Museums of San Francisco	**http://www.thinker.org/**
Time-Life Photo Sight Home Page	**http://www.pathfinder.com/photo/index.html**
USC Interactive Art Museum at the Fisher Gallery	**http://www.usc.edu/org/fishergallery/**
Virtual Library: Museums	**http://www.comlab.ox.ac.uk/archive/other/ museums/lists.html**
WebMuseum	**http://metalab.unc.edu/wm/**

3 Students will want to search subject directories and search engines for materials devoted to their specific artist. It is probably best to begin searching with a subject directory such as Britannica Internet Guide. (**http://www.britannica.com**)

4 Before students begin their searches, you may choose to remind them of some useful search strategies. Names are best searched as phrases. Example: "norman rockwell"

5 Also remind students of use of Boolean operators. Example: "norman rockwell" AND "painting" or "norman rockwell" AND "biography" or +artist+impressionism +history.

6 Students should use print biographical resources, and encyclopedias as well, especially in this exploratory part of the unit.

STRATEGIES:

Present students with the following prompt: You are an artist applying for a prestigious position as the chair of the Art Department at the Virtual University of the Arts. Competition for this position is fierce. There are many great artists applying and you must show your skills as a communicator, as well as your talents as an artist.

■ **ACTIVITY ONE:** Students browse through print sources and art gateway sites in search of an artist whose work they admire. It may help to distribute the List of Famous Artists (attached as Possible Candidates for Chair list).

■ **ACTIVITY TWO:** Students should begin to prepare their storyboards and resumés as they search the Web collecting information on the artist they wish to submit for the university position.

■ **ACTIVITY THREE:** Students create a multimedia presentation about their artist's life and works (see Handout 1).

■ **ACTIVITY FOUR:** At the same time, students use the information they are collecting to prepare a formal resumé and cover letter for their "interview."

■ **ACTIVITY FIVE:** Students present themselves as the chosen artist with teacher, librarian, and class functioning as the interview committee. They should have multiple copies of resumés and cover letters available for all members of the interview committee.

■ **ACTIVITY SIX:** After all presentations, class and teacher discuss and reach agreement on the most impressive artist—the one best qualified to chair the art department.

EVALUATION/CRITIQUE:

Investigation and research will be graded on quality of the products—storyboard, resumé, cover letter and multimedia artist's statement—as well as the oral presentation during the interview/presentation.

(See Task Assessment for Battle of the University Artists.)

COMMENTS/TIPS/FOLLOW-UP:

Teachers may want to focus on particular curricular needs. Artists may be selected from a particular time period or area of the world. I have used this format to fill a position for our department of philosophy as well!

BATTLE OF THE UNIVERSITY ARTISTS: MULTIMEDIA PRESENTATION
(Student Handout 1)

You are an artist applying for the prestigious position of Chair of the Art Department at the Virtual University of the Arts. Competition for this position is fierce. There are many fine artists applying and you must show your skills as a communicator as well as your talents as an artist.

Prepare a multimedia presentation including at least 10 cards, but no more than 20.

Try to convey the message in a manner that enhances the artist's style. Fonts, colors, bullets and other multimedia elements should serve to express the tone, feeling, style and period of the artist.

You should cover all the following in your presentation (remember to think as if you are the artist you choose as a candidate):

■ State your name and the location of your studio.

■ Give a brief statement of your philosophy of art.

■ Give a brief biographical background, and make sure you connect your environment to your work. How did your location, and any historical or social events affect your work?

■ Major influences in the world of art: which artists do you most admire?

■ School(s) of art in which your work fits

■ Predict your lasting influence on the world of art.

■ Judge your choice of your best works.

■ Offer a persuasive argument for your being hired as Chair of the Art Department.

■ Cite all sources including sources of images.

BATTLE OF THE UNIVERSITY ARTISTS: CREATING A RESUMÉ

In real life, you will need to present a resumé whenever you are searching for a job. Because your resumé is often the first impression an employer has of you, it must be carefully prepared. Spelling and grammatical errors are the "kiss of death" in resumé writing. The document should be neat and prepared on high quality paper.

For this project, you are to create a traditional resumé for a famous artist. Try for as much historical accuracy as possible, but be creative. Show off your talents and highlight your career. Brag. Describe the hardships you have had to overcome. Your artist's resume should include but not be limited to:

■ employment objective (Chair of the Art Department at the Virtual University of the Arts)

■ your education

■ employment background

■ awards and honors

■ hobbies and outside interests

 Your word processor may include templates for creating a resumé and cover letter.

You may also visit the following Web sites for additional examples:

Career Help
http://www.myfuture.com/secondary/career.html

CareerBabe Resume Tutorial
http://www.careerbabe.com/restutor.html

Cover Letters: Rensselaer Polytechnic Institute
http://www.rpi.edu/dept/llc/writecenter/web/text/coverltr.html

Monster.com Resumes and Letters
http://content.monster.com/resume/

Quintessential Career and Job-Hunting Resources Guide
http://www.quintcareers.com/

TASK ASSESSMENT LIST FOR BATTLE OF THE UNIVERSITY ARTISTS

	ASSESSMENT POINTS		
	POINTS POSSIBLE	**PEER ASSESSMENT**	**TEACHER ASSESSMENT**

RESUMÉ AND COVER LETTER

1 Student uses proper style for formal letter writing.

2 Opening paragraph of letter "grabs" the reader.

3 Student understands proper resumé format.

4 Information collected is accurate and appropriate for artist.

5 Resumé and letter are attractively presented, free of mechanical errors.

MULTIMEDIA PRESENTATION

1 Thesis is clearly stated.

2 Project is well organized.

3 Strong evidence supports choice of artist. (Each point is supported by appropriate and accurate details)

4 Multimedia elements help convey the message but are not distracting.

5 Conclusion presents a persuasive case for hiring.

6 Student was confident with the information, made eye contact with audience.

7 Presentation: student effectively and creatively communicated research results.

8 Mechanics of writing are followed: correct grammar, spelling and punctuation.

9 Sources are well chosen and well documented.

POSSIBLE CANDIDATES FOR CHAIR OF THE ART DEPARTMENT AT THE VIRTUAL UNIVERSITY OF THE ARTS:

Adams, Ansel (1902-1984)
Angelico, Fra (1400-1445)
Blake, William (1757-1827)
Bosch, Hieronymus (1450-1516)
Botticelli, Sandro (1444-1510)
Brueghel, Pieter the Elder (1525-1569)
Buonarroti, Michelangelo (1475-1564)
Caravaggio, Michelangelo Merisi da (1573-1610)
Cassatt, Mary (1844-1926)
Cezanne, Paul (1839-1906)
Constable, John (1776-1837)
Copley, John Singleton (1738-1815)
Correggio [Antonio Allegri] (1489-1534)
Dali, Salvadore (1904-1989)
David, Jacques-Louis (1748-1825)
De Kooning, Willem (1904-1997)
Delacroix, Eugene (1798-1863)
Eastman, George (1854-1932)
Eakins, Thomas (1844-1916)
El Greco (Domenicos Theotocopoulos) (1541-1614)
Eyck, Jan van (1395-1441)
Gauguin, Paul (1848-1903)
Goya, Francisco (1746-1828)
Hogarth, William (1697-1764)
Homer, Winslow (1836-1910)
Hopper, Edward (1882-1967)
Hughes, Arthur (1832-1915)
Ingres, Jean-Auguste-Dominique (1780-1876)
Johns, Jasper (1930-)
Johnson, William H. (1901-1970)
Kahlo, Frida (1907-1954)
Kandinsky, Wassily (1866-1944)
Klee, Paul (1879-1940)
Koons, Jeff (1955-)
Lawrence, Jacob (1917 -)
Magritte, Rene (1898-1967)
Manet, Edouard (1832-1883)
Max, Peter (1937-)
Miró, Joan (1893-1983)
Modigliani, Amedeo (1884-1920)
Mondrian, Pieter Cornelis (1872-1944)

Monet, Claude (1840-1926)
Moses, Grandma (Mrs. Anna Mary Robertson Moses) (1860-1961)
Munch, Edvard (1863-1944)
O'Keeffe, Georgia (1887-1986)
Parrish, Maxfield (1870-1962)
Picasso, Pablo (1881-1973)
Pissarro, Camille (1830-1903)
Pollock, Jackson (1912-1956)
Raphael (Raffaello Santi) (1483-1520)
Rembrandt (Rembrandt Harmensz van Rijn) (1605-1669)
Remington, Frederic (1861-1909)
Renoir, Pierre-Auguste (1841-1919)
Rivera, Diego (1886-l957)
Rockwell, Norman (1894-1978)
Rossetti, Dante Gabriel (1828-1882)
Rothko, Mark (1903-1970)
Rousseau, Henri (1844-1910)
Rubens, Peter Paul (1577-1640)
Sargent, John Singer (1856-1925)
Schiele, Egon (1890-1918)
Seurat, Georges (1859-1891)
Sisley, Alfred (1839-1899)
Toulouse-Lautrec, Henri de (1864-1901)
Turner, Joseph Mallord William (1775-1851)
Van Gogh, Vincent (1853-1890)
Vecellio, Tiziano "Titian" (1485-1576)
Velazquez, Diego Rodriquez de Silva y (1599-1660)
Vermeer, Jan (1632-1675)
Vernet, Claude-Joseph (1714-1789)
Warhol, Andrew (1928–1987)
Whistler, James Abbott McNeill (1834-1903)
Wood, Grant (1892-1942)
Wyeth, Andrew (1919–   )

TITLE: *Resistance Movements in the Twentieth Century*

AUTHOR: Chris Gentili, Samuels Public Library, Front Royal, Virginia

CURRICULUM AREA: U.S. History

CURRICULUM CONNECTIONS: World History

GRADE LEVELS: 11-12

PREREQUISITES:

- Knowledge of U.S. Bill of Rights
- Familiarity with slavery and Underground Railroad
- Skills in using basic library resource tools (encyclopedias, automated library catalog systems, magazine and newspaper indices, Internet search engines)

INFORMATION LITERACY STANDARDS FOR STUDENT LEARNING:

Standard 2, Indicators 1, 2, 4
Standard 3, Indicators 1-4
Standard 8, Indicator 3

OTHER OUTCOMES/STANDARDS:

The student will be able to compare and contrast the concept of civil disobedience, as illustrated by the Underground Railroad movement in America, to a twentieth century underground resistance movement developed in response to the denial of civil liberties and personal freedoms of individuals.

MATERIALS/SOURCES NEEDED:

- Computers with CD-ROM drive
- Internet access
- Reference books
- Video cameras
- PowerPoint presentation software
- Magazine and newspaper indices or databases
- LCD panel with an overhead projector (optional but very useful)

STRATEGIES:

1 This unit is taught in a two-week time period. It includes two hours of lecture incorporating facilitated discussion for background learning and project assignment.

2 The remainder of the two-week period is devoted to individual research, culminating in presentations during one or two class periods.

3 The strategy for teaching is composed of five phases.

STEPS:

1 Introductory classroom instruction and discussion of assignments

2 Library session identifying library and community resources supporting the assignment, research skill instruction, and practice

3 Individual research

4 Development of the research project

5 Presentations

INSTRUCTIONAL METHODOLOGY:

1 This unit best suits the constructivist theory of learning. Students are taught the concepts and details of the Underground Railroad resistance movement and are then asked to research and apply the salient points of the movement to a modern example of a resistance movement.

2 The methodology for teaching the unit is based on the Big Six research paradigm. Students are given a project with questions that must be addressed for completion. Students are encouraged to utilize various sources of information: personal interviews, reading primary sources from transcripts on radio, internet, books.

3 Research culminates in a creative presentation illustrating the comparison and analysis of the underground movement and a modern resistance movement.

PHASE DESCRIPTIONS:

1 Prior to teaching this unit the library media specialist and teacher must coordinate their respective roles with regard to the expectations, implementation, assistance, and evaluation of the students. This unit is designed as a cooperative effort with the teacher managing the subject content area and library media specialist managing the information skill context area.

2 It is expected that both library media specialist and teacher will assist students in all phases, including evaluation and feedback. The success of this unit relies on the interconnection of the content and information skills expectations for learning.

Phase 1

- Role of teacher: primary class instructor
- Role of library media specialist: planning and executing later phases of unit
- Location: classroom and library
- Objectives: At conclusion of Phase 1, the student will be able to:
  a. describe historical background of the Underground Railroad as an example of civil disobedience.

b. identify examples of similar movements in the twentieth century.

c. describe and comprehend the assignment.

■ METHOD: lecture and discussion

■ CONTENT:

    a. Review background historical information regarding slavery and the Underground Railroad movement and U.S. Bill of Rights

    b. Introduce concepts of civil disobedience in relation to Underground Railroad movement. Introduce salient points of Underground Railroad with regard to questions listed below

    c. Facilitate discussion of examples for similar twentieth-century movements around the world, such as Bosnia, Rwanda, Germany, Russia, Cuba, or Nicaragua.

    d. Introduce assignment: Students will compare and contrast a twentieth-century resistance movement to the Underground Railroad. Students will research the selected twentieth-century movement using at least one print, one electronic and one primary source of information. A bibliography detailing all of the sources used is required. The final presentation must include answers to the following questions:

        What triggered the oppression of the groups?

        Who is assisting the oppressed groups of individuals?

        What freedoms are they seeking?

        If the oppressed are escaping to freedom, how is this being accomplished?

        How has technology aided in communication in modern situations?

        How do the movements relate to each other?

        What punishments will the government apply to those assisting the oppressed?

■ The project can be presented in a variety of formats, for example, interview, PowerPoint presentation, written paper, video news show, or dramatization. Whatever the format, it will be evaluated using the following standards:

    a. Creativity of final presentation along with quality of comparison and analysis of selected twentieth-century movement

    b. Amount of detail in which required questions are answered

    c. Additional questions raised and addressed by the student.

    d. Accuracy of bibliographic format (including citation of all web sites)

    e. Successful meeting of criteria established for use of print, electronic, and primary sources.

Phase 2

■ ROLE OF TEACHER:

    f. Schedule library time; coordinate with library media specialist for entire project.

    g. Facilitate research skill practice.

    h. Clarify assignment detail as needed.

■ ROLE OF LIBRARY MEDIA SPECIALIST: primary instructor for review of research tools, research skills, introduction of new resources, and presentation software skills.

■ LOCATION: library

- **OBJECTIVES:** At conclusion of Phase 2, students will be able to:
    - **i.** Identify a variety of potential sources of information.
    - **j.** Select information appropriate to the problem or question at hand.
    - **k.** Locate the reference section of the library.
    - **l.** Search the Internet or electronic CD-ROM sources listed on the pathfinder.
    - **m.** Search print sources from reference or circulating materials
- **METHOD:** lecture, demonstration, and hands on practice
- **CONTENT:**
    - **n.** Review location of encyclopedias (print and electronic)
    - **o.** Introduce pathfinder for research project and identify access methods.
    - **p.** Demonstrate use of magazine and newspaper databases, both electronic and print.
    - **q.** Review basic Internet browser skills, including Boolean searching; identify search engines and primary sources on the Internet.
    - **r.** Introduce available community resources and their potential use as a resource for final project.
    - **s.** Demonstrate PowerPoint presentation software.
    - **t.** Identify instructional availability of video resources for completion of final project.
    - **u.** Initiate research process and answer questions; facilitate use of research tools.

Phase 3
- **ROLE OF TEACHER:**
    - **a.** Assist student with research process and project development.
    - **b.** Clarify expectations, suggest products and formats, and answer project content questions.
- **ROLE OF LIBRARY MEDIA SPECIALIST:** Assist with student research process with regard to resource tools and format for presentations.
- **LOCATION:** library
- **OBJECTIVES:** At the conclusion of Phase 3, the student will have a presentation for review which will include:
    - **c.** rough draft of the final project completed.
    - **d.** written outline of project a description of the final project format with sources identified.
    - **e.** evidence that questions in Phase 1 are addressed as well as continuing to compare and contrast movements.
- **METHOD:** Independent research
- **CONTENT:**
    - **f.** Both library media specialist and teacher will reinforce use of electronic and print resources, Internet sites.
    - **g.** Clarify final project requirements; confirm that required questions are being addressed in the project.

Phase 4

■ **ROLE OF TEACHER:** Assist student with project completion relative to content.

■ **ROLE OF LIBRARY MEDIA SPECIALIST:** Assist student with project completion relative to process.

■ **LOCATION:** library or classroom

■ **OBJECTIVE:** At the end of Phase 4, the project will be completed and ready for presentation.

■ **METHOD:** Independent presentation

■ **CONTENT:**

    a. Continue to utilize all available resources in library to help students with presentations, including video taping, Power Point presentation, word processing, and bibliographic content.

    b. Continue to assist students regarding meeting the content requirements of project.

Phase 5

■ **ROLE OF TEACHER:** evaluate projects according to academic and format content requirements.

■ **ROLE OF LIBRARY MEDIA SPECIALIST:** evaluate projects according to established information literacy standards and criteria

■ **LOCATION:** library or classroom.

■ **OBJECTIVES:**

    c. Presentation of projects to class, teachers and library media specialist

    d. Evaluation and feedback by both teacher and library media specialist

■ **CONTENT:** Projects are assessed by the teacher and library media specialist regarding original objectives and level at which these are met.

EVALUATION:

Both the teacher and library media will use Information Power and content standards to evaluate projects:

■ Students must submit a bibliography, typed according to locally adopted format, including at least one electronic, print, and primary source.

■ Students must have answered the questions listed in Phase 1.

■ The originality of the final product will be measured by content and as a reflection of Information Power Standard 3 (all indicators) and objectives for historical analysis.

PATHFINDER FOR CIVIL DISOBEDIENCE RESEARCH PROJECT

The following research tools will guide you in your search for information about resistance movements:

ENCYCLOPEDIAS

- Use these for basic reference starting points about countries, resistance movements during World War II, and famous people in government.
- **PRINT:** *World Book, Encyclopedia Americana, Encyclopedia Britannica*
- **CD-ROM:** Encarta, World Book, Groliers

MAGAZINE AND NEWSPAPER INDEXES

- **PRINT:** Use the *Reader's Guide to Periodical Literature* for current articles in magazines about your topic; the index will refer you to specific magazines and articles. If the magazines are not available at the school library, check your local public library.
- **CD-ROM DATABASES:** Use Infotrac or ProQuest for magazine articles in hundreds of magazines on CD-ROM.
- **INTERNET:** Use Electric Library for newspaper and magazine articles. For newspaper articles online start with the following: **AJR Newslink: http://www.ajr.org**

WEB SITES

- National Resistance movements: **http://www.webcom.com/hrin/resist.html**
- United Nations High Commission for Human Rights: **http://www.unhchr.ch/**
- Use other search engines as discussed in class with the search methods outlined in the rubric to find other sites related to your topic.

BOOKS

In the catalog, search some of the following topics:

- resistance movements
- underground resistance movements
- Underground Railroad
- genocide

Depending on your topic, search for specific country or name of movement, such as "France" or "French resistance movement."

Collaborating in the Learning Process

By Alice Yucht

STANDARD 9: The student who contributes positively to the learning community and to society is information literate and participates effectively in groups to pursue and generate information.

According to *Information Power: Building Partnerships for Learning*, the student who meets this standard demonstrates the skills at the heart of being an effective information consumer. He or she "seeks and shares information and ideas across a range of sources and perspectives, . . . acknowledges the insights and contributions of a variety of cultures and disciplines . . . collaborates with diverse individuals to identify information problems," and can "communicate these solutions accurately and creatively" (*Information Power*, p. 39). Each of the four indicators for Standard 9, from

"shares information with others" to "collaboratively designs complex products in a variety of formats," builds on the previous one and involves more complex information literacy skills.

Each of the indicators includes three levels of proficiency, reflecting an increased awareness of the value of working with others for the greater good of all. At the most primary level we see this happen every day, whether it's kindergartners turning pages and saying, "oooh, look!" to their fellow browsers, or high schoolers e-mailing Web site addresses to each other. At the more advanced levels, we watch (sometimes in awe) as student teams create elaborate online presentations to extend the classroom curriculum or expand personal knowledge of a subject. Demonstration of even the basic levels of proficiency for each indicator would still be considered evidence of a successful student; achievement of higher levels of proficiency is the pinnacle we strive for.

Indicator 1, "Shares knowledge and information with others," reiterates the foundational premise of *Information Power:* "building partnerships for learning." At the most basic level, students merely contribute to the "group efforts by seeking and communicating specific facts, opinions, and points of view." At the exemplary level, they all work together to integrate each "one's own knowledge and information with that of others in the group."

Indicator 2, "Respects others' ideas and backgrounds and acknowledges their contributions," begins with the development of adequate note-taking skills as a prerequisite for the basic proficiency of being able to "describe others' ideas accurately and completely." At the exemplary level, they help to "organize and integrate the contributions of all members of the group into information products." This skill is amply demonstrated in the "Mathematician Biographies" activity by Allison Bernstein. Here students work in pairs to research a mathematician's life and work, and then use PowerPoint to present their findings (including pictures and maps) to the class.

Indicator 3 requires more complex skills, as the student "collaborates with others, both in person and through technologies, to identify information problems and to seek their solutions." At the most Basic level, "express(ing) one's own ideas appropriately and effectively...to identify and resolve information

> **Our connection to the learning community, both locally and globally, "provides a bridge between formal, school-based learning and independent, lifelong learning."**

problems" could include sending an e-mail request for help with a question to ICONnect or Ask-an-Expert. The Proficient student "participates actively in discussions with others, in person and remotely through technologies, to analyze information problems and to suggest solutions." Such discussions could be in traditional class forums, through electronic communication formats such as chat rooms or listservs, or as part of online learning activities such as the Butterfly Project that requires ongoing participation by students from all over the world.

At the Exemplary level, the student "participates actively in discussions with others, in person and remotely through technologies, to devise solutions to information problems that integrate group members' information and ideas." Here the student is not just gathering and comparing information, but using the discussions about this information to analyze results in order to solve problems.

"The Disabilities Webpage Project" by Lesley Farmer demonstrates how students can work together—each taking on a different production role in order to produce a unified information product reflecting all of their efforts. The topic selected for this particular collaborative project can also help open students' eyes to the differences they encounter in the world around them.

In Indicator 4, the student "collaborates with others, both in person and through technologies, to design, develop, and evaluate information products and solutions" that provide new knowledge and further insights for the group. At the basic level, the student "works with others, in person and remotely through technologies, to create and evaluate simple information products." This could be a poster, a puzzle, or skit based on the information gathered. Mary Alice Anderson and Kate O'Grady suggest student collaborative groups work together to create a prototype space exploration vehicle in "Mission to Mars." This is the kind of project that can lead to spectacular examples of teamwork and creativity as students become engaged in problem-solving and decision-making activities.

Joyce Valenza's "Which U.S. President Did the Most To Promote Civil Rights?" activity demonstrates the highest level of achievement for this indicator, as students "create and evaluate complex information products that integrate information in a variety of formats." For this project, students need to know how to search for and synthesize a variety of information sources, state a thesis and defend a position based on evidence; examine and use primary source materials as evidence; develop an effective, persuasive multimedia presentation; then finally evaluate all of the presentations in order to vote for a single "winner."

Standard 9 reflects not only the fundamental goals of every school library program, but also the National Study of School Evaluation's "Schoolwide Goals for Student Learning" based on the *Indicators of Schools of Quality* (*Information Power,* Appendix D, pp.171-72). These goals include learning-to-learn skills, the ability to expand and integrate knowledge, communication skills utilizing both print and electronic formats, higher-order thinking and reasoning skills, interpersonal skills, and a recognition of personal and social responsibility to the community. An effective school library program recognizes and supports the values inherent in all of these goals. Our connection to the learning community, both locally and globally, "provides a bridge between formal, school-based learning and independent, lifelong learning" (*Information Power,* p.122). Because school librarians are not bound to any one subject or grade level, we have both the opportunity and the responsibility to make sure that our students are adequately prepared to become effective as both information consumers and producers in the ever-expanding information universe.

Alice H. Yucht is a Teacher-Librarian at Heritage Middle School in Livingston, New Jersey.

TITLE: *Mathematician Biographies*

AUTHOR: Allison Bernstein, Library Media Specialist, Dale Street School, Medfield, Massachusetts

CURRICULUM AREA: Mathematics

CURRICULUM CONNECTIONS: Social Studies

GRADE LEVEL: 8

PREREQUISITES: None

INFORMATION LITERACY STANDARDS FOR STUDENT LEARNING:
Standard 3, Indicators 1, 4
Standard 9, Indicators 1-4

OTHER OUTCOMES/STANDARDS:
BIG6:

- Students will, working in pairs, choose a famous mathematician from a list provided by the Library Media Specialist.

- Upon choosing a mathematician, students will research the mathematician's life and work, following the handout provided. Using PowerPoint, they will present their findings (including pictures and maps) to the class.

- Students will gain a deeper understanding of the math concepts as they research, as well as developing group work skills and presentation techniques.

MATERIALS/SOURCES NEEDED:

- List of mathematicians arranged by their birthdate (month and day). Sources will depend upon site collection.

- Access to Internet with bookmarked sites about mathematicians and current reference books with biographical information

- Electronic encyclopedias or atlases

- Scanner or digital camera for print only sources

- Group presentation computer screen

STRATEGIES:

- The classroom teacher and Library Media Specialist together give students an overview of the project.

- Each pair of students is told they will be researching a mathematician and presenting their findings in a PowerPoint presentation. Students will initially choose a mathematician by matching their own birth month with that of a mathematician. Since students are working in pairs, it is best to try to pair students with the same birth month. If this is not possible, the pair will have to select one mathematician for the project.

- Each of the handouts is reviewed, with special attention given to instructions for using software programs.

- Demonstration of the software is provided, and a modeling of the final product is used for an example. Demonstration should highlight components of presentation students will need to produce, such as pictures from the WWW, excerpts from encyclopedias, or print material. After demonstration, direct students to research sources.

- A work-cited sheet will be completed. Students should be reminded that all information gathered will be utilized in some way in the presentation.

- At this point, it should also be made clear that no pair will begin work on their presentation before all research is complete. This will prevent students from sitting at the computer with an open book, or alternating between a Web page and their presentation, which invites plagiarism.

- Each pair is given a folder in which to keep all of their research. The folder will be collected at the end of the project for evaluation.

- After the pairs have completed their research, they will follow the PowerPoint outline and create their presentation. Remind students to check spelling, facts, and balance of effects and content.

- Students will present their PowerPoint programs to the class. Students should be reminded not to read off the screen, but to use it as an outline. While the presentations are given, the teacher and Library Media Specialist use an assessment rubric for evaluation. Factor into final evaluation the manner in which the pair worked together to complete the research.

EVALUATION/CRITIQUE:

The assessment rubric will be completed by teacher and Library Media Specialist.

- Rubric should contain a checklist of required components, as well as use of presentation software and creativity of presentation, including an item evaluating how well the students transitioned between slides. The map, picture, contributions, history, name, and dates function as a checklist for components of the project.

- This assessment item is just one part of the evaluation. Rubric, folders, and observations will all be taken into account for the final grade. The folder should contain all completed research sheets (including the work-cited sheet) as well as any pictures or maps scanned.

COMMENTS/TIPS/FOLLOW-UP:

- Students may need an introduction to the WWW and navigation of Web sites. If pairs finish creating their presentation early, they can serve as extra trainers for those students having difficulty.

- Inviting parents in for final presentations is a good way to showcase students' abilities, as well as resources and learning opportunities found in the Library Media Center. If the local paper can't come to take pictures, send some; it's a great way to generate positive PR for your library.

GETTING STARTED WITH POWER POINT

STUDENT OVERVIEW:

- Choose NEW PRESENTATION.
- Select the presentation design of your choice.
- Choose a layout for your slide.
- Click in the areas for text and start typing. (Animation effects can be used here: highlight the words you want the effect to be used on.)
- To add in a picture, double click for clip art or click once to add a picture from a disk. You will be getting other pictures from the A: drive.
- TOOLS: Slide Transition. Choose effects you would like to use for transitions between slides.
- Choose NEW SLIDE and continue working on your presentation.
- When you are finished, choose FILE: Save as: and save your presentation to the A: drive (make sure there is a disk in there). Name your presentation.

Name:_____

Date::_____

Class::_____

MATHEMATICIANS RESEARCH

Name:_____

Birthday_____

Born (Place)_____

Died (Place and Date) _____

Famous in what field?_____

Renowned for study, discovery, or development of _____

_____

_____

What impact did this have on their field of study? _____

_____

Were there any historically significant events taking place during your mathematician's life?
_____

_____

Other interesting or important facts about your mathematician? _____

_____

Find a picture of your mathematician (photo or drawing is acceptable).

Find a map of his/her country of origin.

ELECTRONIC MATHEMATICIANS' SOURCES:

Internet (many other sources available):

http://www-groups.dcs.st-and.ac.uk/~history/Indexes/

http://www.agnesscott.edu/lriddle/women/women.htm

PRINT SOURCES:

Bell, *Men of Mathematics.* Simon and Schuster, 1986.

Biographical Dictionary of Scientists. Oxford University Press, 1994.

Dunham, *Journey Through Genius: The Great Theoremos of Mathematics.* Wiley, 1990.
    Math and Mathematicians, 2 vol. UXL, 1999.

Dunham, *The Mathematical Universe.* Wiley, 1999.

Henderson, *Modern Mathematicians.* Facts on File, 1996.

*Lives and Legacies—An Encyclopedia of People Who Changed the World: Scientists,
    Mathematicians, and Inventors.* Oryx Press, 1999.

Notable Mathematicians: From Ancient Times to the Present. Gale Research, 1999

Notable Women in Mathematics: A Biographical Dictionary. Greenwood Press, 1998.

Perl, *Math Equals: Biographies of Women Mathematicians & Related Activities.*
    Addison-Wesley, 1978.

Reimer, *Mathematicians are People Too, Vol. 1: Stories from the Lives of Great
    Mathematicians.* Dale Seymour Publications, 1990.

Reimer, *Mathematicians are People Too, Vol. 2: Stories from the Lives of Great
    Mathematicians.* Dale Seymour Publications, 1995

Yount, *A to Z of Women in Science and Math.* Facts on File, 1999.

Yount, *Contemporary Women Scientists.* Facts on File, 1994

TITLE: *Mission to Mars*

AUTHORS: Mary Alice Anderson, Library Media Specialist; Kate O'Grady, Teacher; Winona (Minnesota) Middle School

CURRICULUM AREAS: Earth science

CURRICULUM CONNECTIONS: Math

GRADE LEVELS: 8-10

PREREQUISITES: Internet navigation skills, basic search skills, collaborative group work skills

INFORMATION LITERACY STANDARDS FOR STUDENT LEARNING:
Standard 3, Indicators 3, 4
Standard 9, Indicators 1-4

CONTENT STANDARD:
The students will learn about features of Mars.

MATERIALS/SOURCES NEEDED:
- Internet, NASA web site (**http://www.NASA.gov**)
- Online resources such as magazines, encyclopedia, *Newsbank Science Source* database
- Current books on Mars
- Science encyclopedias and dictionaries
- Computer projection system
- Paper, cardboard, wire, coloring supplies, or any "vehicle construction" supplies the students may want to use (can be supplied by students, teacher or library media specialist as needed)

STRATEGIES:

1 Students must design and build a prototype model for a robotic vehicle for use in gathering information from Mars.

2 Students work in collaborative groups of three, and each group receives a specific task. Groups are asked to design a vehicle to complete that task while exploring Mars. No humans are allowed on the exploration. They do not have to explain in detail how the vehicle works, but they need to design a vehicle that can do the job. The collaborative groups prepare a project report.

3 Science teacher introduces the project in the classroom. Students are given a current document about the exploration of Mars (from a news magazine, a science magazine, or the NASA Web site).

4 Students are asked to answer questions pertaining to the article (this helps give them all a similar background).

5 As a group (with the image projected on a large screen in the classroom) the students explore the NASA Web site to learn about future missions. This activity helps all students become familiar with the NASA Web site.

6 Students begin their research in the media center. The library media specialist reviews or introduces key resources for finding current information. The level of instruction needed will depend on previous earth science research projects. Students are reminded to pay attention to copyright dates in materials and to focus on materials that are the most current. Use science encyclopedias and other books for background information.

7 Sample tasks for the vehicle can include going to the polar ice cap region, making a map of cap distribution, drilling samples, analyzing the ice samples, and going to Ares Vallis region of Mars to collect soil samples for a microscopic analysis.

STEPS:

The research process has four phases:

Question: understand your tasks.

1 Research: Collect background information, prepare a list of needed instruments, and define the abilities of your vehicle

2 Planning: prepare initial sketches of vehicle and, as a team, decide on final plan and specifications of vehicle.

3 Building: construct the vehicle.

4 Reporting: write the project report according to above guidelines.

The reporting phase is a roundtable presentation. One team member stays with the vehicle and other students move around the room listening to presentations about all of the vehicles. In the second round, students shift and another person does the presentation.

EVALUATION/CRITIQUE:

A scoring system is used to evaluate both the vehicle and the group presentation.
Vehicle is evaluated on:

■ Appropriate name	1 point
■ Scale (for example: 1 inch = ___miles)	1 point
■ Legend (key and labels)	2 points
■ Brief summary card describing the vehicle	2 points
■ Actual model	9 points

Project report is evaluated on:

■ Purpose of the mission	2 points
■ Instruments vehicle used	2 points
■ How vehicle is powered	2 points
■ How vehicle is controlled	2 points
■ How vehicle will overcome potential difficulties and dangers of Martian environment (irregular surface rocks, dust and wind storms, extreme temperatures)	2 points
■ agencies and or sponsoring mission	1 point
■ name group has given the vehicle	1 point
■ revisions made in vehicle during the research process	2 points

PEER COLLABORATIVE GROUP WORK ASSESSMENT:

Rating scale

3: Contributed fair share AND was a good, cooperative group member
2: Contributed fair share but was noncooperative OR was cooperative but did not contribute fair share of workload
1: Contributed very little AND was not very cooperative with others
0: Did nothing or actually detracted from group work

Everyone should rank the group members (including themselves) individually.

Member 1 _____	Member 2_____	Member 3_____
Rating 1 _____	_____	_____
Rating 2 _____	_____	_____
Rating 3 _____	_____	_____
Teacher _____	_____	_____
Average _____	_____	_____

Total score _____

COMMENTS/TIPS/FOLLOW-UP:

The Mission to Mars project involves research, hands on learning, and collaborative group work.
The project should be fun, making research fun.!

TITLE: *Disabilities Web Pages*

AUTHOR: Lesley S. J. Farmer, Associate Professor, California State University, Long Beach, California

CURRICULUM AREA: Health

CURRICULUM CONNECTION: Social Studies, Information Skills

PREREQUISITES: Experience in using searching tools, basic Web page development (at least one person in a group)

GRADE LEVELS: 9-12

INFORMATION LITERACY STANDARDS FOR STUDENT LEARNING:
Standard 2, Indicators 1, 4
Standard 3, Indicators 1, 4
Standard 9, Indicators 1-4

OTHER OUTCOMES/STANDARDS:
BIG6: Information seeking strategies/Select the best sources
- Students will be able to select the best sources of information about disabilities and adaptive technology.

Location and Access/Locate sources/Find information within the source
- Students will be able to locate and select information about disabilities and adaptive technology.
- Students will be able to locate images about disabilities and adaptive technology.

Use of Information/Extract relevant information
- Students will be able to analyze information to make inferences about disabilities and achievements.

Synthesis/organize information from multiple sources, present the information
- Students will be able to scan and import images into Web format.
- Students will be able to present findings in Web format.
- Students will be able to create a Web page about disabilities.

MATERIALS/SOURCES NEEDED:
- Sources on disabilities and adaptive technology (print and electronic)
- Computer with Web authoring software

STRATEGIES:

- Library Media Specialist discusses the tern *disabilities* and relates it to the word *handicapped*, since both words are used as key terms. Emphasize the fact that people have disabilities, but are not disabilities themselves.
- Students brainstorm about famous people with disabilities. Because some students may have difficulty identifying people, encourage the class to share good sources of information.
- Explain the term *adaptive technology*, and give a couple of examples (scanners, special keyboards). Also mention older adaptations, such as Braille books and wheelchairs.
- As students create Web pages about disabilities, encourage them to select clear and relevant images.

STEPS:

- Students are put into small cooperative groups of three to four and must divide up the tasks equitably.
- Each group chooses a disability.
- Each group finds and extracts information about a famous person with that disability and the person's means of dealing with the disability, particularly the use of adaptive aids or technology.
- Each group locates images to place on a Web page, such as a photo or illustration of their person, the disability, and any adaptive aids used.
- Each groups creates their own Web page, incorporating their images and synthesized findings from research.

WRAP UP:

- Students compare Web pages in terms of disabilities portrayed and adaptive technologies used.
- Library Media Specialist can help students generalize this research approach to other topics.

EVALUATION/CRITIQUE :

- Groups evaluate their peers' Web pages in terms of accuracy, thoroughness, and presentation quality.
- Class draws conclusions about disabilities, which should be assessed for accuracy and insight.

COMMENTS/TIPS/FOLLOW-UP:

- Students may feel uncomfortable about discussing disabilities, especially if a student in the group has significant disabilities. Mutual respect is of paramount importance. Students may want to interview a person with disabilities during this project or try out some adaptive technology themselves.
- This is a good activity to do in small cooperative groups. Only one student out of four needs to know how to create a Web page; others can be design experts, word processors, or scanners to divide up the technology skills.
- Current word processing programs often can be saved as HTML documents. The project is most successful if students can "publish" their pages on the Internet, so preparation may be needed to find a way to have these pages online or to be seen as "online ready."
- Students should discuss copyright issues in terms of Web publishing and be scrupulous in crediting graphics as well as source information.

BIBLIOGRAPHY OF ELECTRONIC SOURCES:

Yahoo lists several relevant sites under Business and Economy: Assistive Technology
**http://dir.yahoo.com/Business_and_Economy/Companies/Disabilities/Assistive_Tech
nology/**

The Adaptive Technology Resource Center at the University of Toronto
http://www.utoronto.ca/atrc/

EASI: Equal Access to Software and Information
http://www.rit.edu/~easi/

National Council on Disability
http://www.ncd.gov/

WebABLE!
http://www.yuri.org/webable/index.html

TITLE: *Which U.S. President Did the Most to Promote Civil Rights?*

AUTHOR: Joyce Kasman Valenza, Librarian, Springfield Township (Pennsylvania) High School

BACKGROUND:

■ A group of civil rights organizations recently met to establish an award to be presented in honor of the United States President who made the greatest contribution to promoting civil rights in our country.

■ The charge is to research and present the cases for the most worthy candidates. Students are responsible for presenting the credentials of one worthy president to representatives of the committee.

CURRICULUM AREA: Social Studies

CURRICULUM CONNECTIONS: Language Arts, Information Skills

GRADE LEVELS: 8-12 (may be adapted for younger students)

PREREQUISITES:

■ An understanding of the use of primary sources in historical research

■ Some background in United States history

■ An understanding of the concept 'civil rights'.

INFORMATION LITERACY STANDARDS FOR STUDENT LEARNING:

Standard 3, Indicators 1, 3, 4
Standard 5, Indicator 3
Standard 9, Indicators 1, 3, 4

OTHER OUTCOMES/STANDARDS:

■ Students will sort through biographical and primary source material to evaluate presidential accomplishments in the area of civil rights.

■ Students will search for and synthesize a variety of information sources .

■ Students will improve Web searching skills.

■ Students will state a thesis and defend a position based on evidence.

■ Students will examine and use primary source materials as evidence.

■ Students will develop an effective, persuasive multimedia presentation.

MATERIALS/SOURCES NEEDED:

- Microsoft Word or other word processing package for creating tables
- Power Point, Hyperstudio or other multimedia authoring program for presentation project
- Web browser and Internet connection
- Additional print and video resources related to the presidents
- Style sheet for bibliographic citation
- Group presentation equipment for student projects

WEB RESOURCES:

See list on student handout.

STRATEGIES:

ACTIVITY 1: Introduction (half a class period)

- Library Media Specialist begins discussion about which presidents would be possible choices for award. Record names of suggested presidents on the board.
- Discuss criteria for determining level of a president's commitment to civil rights issues. How can we judge a president on these issues? Brainstorm some of the specific criteria and record on board.

ACTIVITY TWO: Preliminary Research (one to two class periods)

- Library Media Specialist divides class into groups of four or five students.
- Library Media Specialist explains tasks and reminds students they will be evaluated on the basis of their organizers/scaffolds, their group work, and their final presentations.

STEPS:

1 Each student group reaches consensus on a definition on the term *civil rights*.

2 Group creates a chart for preliminary research which includes three presidents the group believes are most worthy of the award and the criteria believed most effective in analyzing their contributions. (See Preliminary Organizer or ask students to develop their own charts.) The chart may include some of the criteria brainstormed by the class. Each group may develop additional criteria as they confer and research.

3 Students search Internet and print materials for primary and secondary source evidence to support the worthiness of each of the three Presidents.

4 Students should begin their research with the group of selected Web sites but may expand their search to subject directories and search engines. Before they begin searching you may choose to remind them of some useful search strategies:

Examples: Names and phrases are best searched as phrases

"civil rights" AND "president kennedy" or
"civil rights" AND "john f. kennedy"

Also remind students of syntax differences between search engines:

+"civil rights" +kennedy

5 Each group should reach consensus and select one of the researched presidents as a focus for their final research and presentation.

ACTIVITY THREE: Final research (two class periods)
STEPS:

1 Groups create a new chart specifically designed to collect information about one president. This chart will become an outline for the group's multimedia presentation (see Final Organizer).

2 Collect information for all criteria selected.

3 Conclusion on chart should strongly defend president's worthiness for this prestigious civil rights award.

ACTIVITY FOUR: Multimedia production (four class periods)
STEPS:

Student groups create a multimedia presentation comprised of at least 10 but no more than 20 slides, which are aimed at persuading the committee of the worthiness of chosen President. Slides should include the following:

Opening card stating name of president and names of the group members.

■ Statement of thesis, briefly explaining why the president selected is most worthy for the award.

■ At least three pieces of evidence, using at least two cards, to develop each point. Include primary sources to support this evidence.

■ Concluding slide should strongly state why this president is the most worthy.

■ Last card(s) must be a work cited card and must note the Web sites and other sources from which both textual information and images were gathered.

ACTIVITY FIVE: Student presentations (two to three class periods)

ACTIVITY SIX: Reaching a conclusion (half a class period)

■ Library Media Specialist leads class discussion to determine which president should receive the award. Students should refer to specific evidence presented by the groups in their comments

■ End the unit with a vote for the most worthy candidate to recommend to the award committee.

EVALUATION/CRITIQUE:

■ Checkpoints: Students' in-process work will be evaluated using the organizers for collecting presidential information.

■ Final product: Students' final work will be assessed through their multimedia presentation (see Task Assessment List for evaluating the presidents).

COMMENTS/TIPS/FOLLOW-UP:

Teachers may choose to focus on presidents of a particular decade or century. This project may be adapted for younger students by broadening its focus. Have students select the "best" president by first establishing criteria they believe will help them make their choice.

WHICH U.S. PRESIDENT DID THE MOST TO PROMOTE CIVIL RIGHTS?
Student Handout

A group of civil rights organizations recently met to establish an award to be presented in honor of the United States President who has made the greatest contribution to promoting civil rights in our country. Your charge is to research and present a case for the most worthy candidates. You are responsible for presenting the credentials of one worthy president to representatives of the committee.

YOUR GROUP'S TASKS:

1 Select three possible presidents and explore their worthiness for this award. You will do this by creating a chart to help you examine primary and secondary source evidence relating to the three presidents you select.

2 Based on that preliminary research, select one president on which your group will focus. Create a chart to help you examine specific evidence relating to this president's qualifications.

3 Create a multimedia presentation comprised of at least 10 but no more than 20 slides to persuade the committee why your president deserves the new Civil Rights award.

YOUR SLIDES SHOULD INCLUDE THE FOLLOWING:

■ Opening card stating the name of your president and the names of the group members.

■ Statement of thesis. Briefly state why the President you selected is most worthy for the award.

■ Select at least three pieces of evidence, using at least two cards to develop each point. Include primary sources to support this evidence.

■ Your concluding slide should clinch it for the committee; your president is indeed the most worthy!

■ You last card must be a work cited card and must note Web sites and other sources from which both textual information and images were gathered.

YOU MAY FIND THESE WEB SITES HELPFUL IN YOUR RESEARCH:

American Presidency (Grolier online)
http://gi.grolier.com/presidents/ea/ea_toc.html

The American Experience: The Presidents
http://www.pbs.org/wgbh/pages/amex/presidents/indexjs.html

Inaugural Addresses of the Presidents
http://www.bartleby.com/124/index.html

American Presidents: Life Portraits
http://www.americanpresidents.org/

POTUS (Presidents of the United States)
http://www.ipl.org/ref/POTUS

Speeches of United States Presidents
http://www.ocean.ic.net/rafiles/pres/thelist.html

Presidents of the United States
http://www.whitehouse.gov/WH/glimpse/presidents/html/presidents.html

National Portrait Gallery Hall of Presidents
http://www.npg.si.edu/col/pres/

Celebrating Democracy
http://artsedge.kennedy-center.org/celeb/celeb.html

President (includes Presidential Libraries Web, Web sites for all Presidents, and First Ladies)
http://metalab.unc.edu/lia/president/

Presidential Debates History
http://www.netcapitol.com/history.htm

US Presidents Lists
http://www.fujisan.demon.co.uk/USPresidents/preslist.htm

PRELIMINARY ORGANIZER FOR PRESIDENTIAL AWARD

	PRESIDENT 1	PRESIDENT 2	PRESIDENT 3
Speeches			
Legislation			
Appointments			
Quotes			
News/Historical Events during term			
Other Criteria			
Evaluation (Is this President the most worthy?)			

FINAL ORGANIZER FOR PRESIDENTIAL AWARD

	SELECTED PRESIDENT_____
Criterion 1	
Criterion 2	
Criterion 3	
Conclusion	

TASK ASSESSMENT LIST FOR PRESIDENTIAL AWARD

ASSESSMENT POINTS

	POINTS POSSIBLE	PEER ASSESSMENT	TEACHER ASSESSMENT

PRELIMINARY ORGANIZER

1 An appropriate list of criteria was selected.

2 Appropriate presidents were selected for comparison.

3 Information collected was accurate and appropriate.

4 Data were collected from credible sources.

5 Data were well organized in chart form.

FINAL ORGANIZER

1 Group chose appropriate criteria for examining the contributions of selected President .

2 Information collected was accurate and appropriate.

3 Data were collected from credible sources.

4 Data were well organized in chart form.

5 Group has selected effective quotes for presentation.

6 Logical conclusion was reached based on evidence collected.

MULTIMEDIA PRESENTATION

1 Thesis was clearly stated.

2 Project was well organized.

3 Strong evidence supports choice of president.

4 Each point supported by appropriate and accurate details.

5 Quotations are effectively used.

6 Multimedia elements helped convey message and were not distracting.

_____ _____ _____

7 Conclusion was persuasive.

_____ _____ _____

8 Sources were well-documented.

_____ _____ _____

9 Mechanics of writing were followed: grammar, spelling, punctuation.

_____ _____ _____

10 Group members worked effectively to produce the product.

_____ _____ _____

11 Presentation: Group effectively communicated the results of their research to their audience.

_____ _____ _____

12 Group was clearly familiar with material. Speakers maintained eye contact, spoke clearly and persuasively.

_____ _____ _____

DATE DUE

APR 1 1 2001		
APR 1 6 REC'D		
SEP 05 2001		
COMPLETED SEP 2 0 2001		
MAR 1 4 2002		
REC'D APR 0 1 2002		
APR 2 6 2004 RECEIVED APR 2 6 2004		
OCT 2 4 2005		
MAR 1 0 2006		
REC'D OCT 2 4 2005		
REC'D MAR 1 0 2006		